Raiment

Also by Jan Kemp

Against the Softness of Woman, Caveman Press, Dunedin, 1976

Diamonds and Gravel, Hampson Hunt, Wellington, 1979

The Other Hemisphere, Three Continents Press, Washington DC, and Butterfly Books, Sydney, 1991

The Sky's Enormous Jug: Love Poems Old and New, Puriri Press, Auckland, 2001

Only One Angel, Otago University Press, Dunedin, 2001

Dante's Heaven, Puriri Press, Auckland, 2006

Voicetracks, Puriri Press, Auckland, and Tranzlit, Kronberg im Taunus, 2012

Il Cielo di Dante, Edizione del Poggio, Poggio Imperiale, 2016

Dante Down Under, Tranzlit, Kronberg im Taunus, 2017

Spirals of Breath, Tranzlit, Kronberg im Taunus, 2019

Black Ice & the Love Planet / Schwarzes Eis & der Planet der Liebe, Tranzlit, Kronberg im Taunus, 2020

Tripstones, Puriri Press, Auckland, 2020; Tranzlit, Kronberg im Taunus, 2021

From here to there . . . a journey to the Antipodes with Dante Alighieri, https://vimeo.com/605045006; https://vimeo/604914170, 2021

Raiment

A Memoir

Jan Kemp

MASSEY UNIVERSITY PRESS

In memory of my parents,
who gave me life.

Joan Anne Kemp, née Hooton, 1920–2001

Morice Harold Kemp, 1905–1988

'And why take ye thought for raiment? Consider the lilies of the field, how they grow; they toil not, neither do they spin; And yet I say unto you that Solomon in all his glory was not arrayed like one of these.'

— Matthew 6:28–29

Author's note

The names of many friends, family members, public figures and teachers who appear in this book have been retained, but some names have been changed or abbreviated for reasons of privacy.

Contents

1949

—

1961

1.

Before I can remember, I am born on 12 March 1949 in the maternity ward at Campbell Johnstone Hospital in Claudelands, Hamilton. My mother Joan is almost twenty-nine, and my father Morice in his forty-fourth year. A few months later I'm flown to Christchurch with Joan for an operation to stitch my split upper lip. Luckily, I don't have a cleft palate, which would have made speech difficult.

I'm baptised on 13 August by Harald Heaslip, the vicar at St Aidan's Church in Claudelands, with Mum's best friend Wendy, her husband Jackson Madill, and Betty Turbott, another close friend of Joan's, becoming my godparents. Dorothy and Arthur Hooton, my maternal grandparents, and my eighteen-months-older brother Peter, as well as Garth Turbott are also present at my baptism. Betty must have taken the photos afterwards in the front garden of the Kemp house in Bains Avenue, Claudelands.

A year later my father is offered a job in Morrinsville. There the family settles into a large bungalow on a quarter-acre section with an orchard at 21 Alexandra Avenue.

I can see the dark panelling of the drawing room, the paisley-patterned carpet, hear my parents' voices outside as Pete and I run to the front door behind Nanny, who opens it. *Can we see Iwi, can we see Iwi?* we chant as our mother steps in through the door usually used only for visitors. She's cradling an armful. Our father follows, carrying her little brown suitcase. He's smiling too. She bends down, lowering the bundle, and she shows us our new brother, and we hold his finger and say *Hello Iwi*. He smells like warm milk. He has blond fluff on his head and huge blue eyes. We love him instantly.

Now there are three of us. Peter is nearly five and a half. I, Janet, am four years and two months, and Iwi (we cannot pronounce Ian) was born today. It is 8 May 1953. We don't know that Queen Elizabeth II is about to be crowned. We don't know that Iwi was born on the eighth anniversary of VE Day, or that *iwi* means bone, nation, strength.

Pete takes me to my first day at kindy on his red scooter. I stand behind, holding him round the waist with one hand, and he stands on his right leg, holding the stick handlebars, and scoots with his left foot. In my other hand I hold the leather strap of a little square tin box containing my lunch and playlunch. We come to a stop by a big tree outside the Anglican church hall, and in I go.

Pete is my best friend. He can suddenly waft away from you like a puff of dandelion and you know he's gone inside his own thoughts. So, you just say *Pete!* and he's back. He always has ideas about what we can do. Once Mum was telling us off when we'd been naughty and he said, *Come on Jan, let's go.* So, we went. Mum was just left there. It was rude of us, but she laughed later and said not to tease her. Another time, to show her how much she talked when her friends were there, he took away his milk glass when she wasn't looking at it but at the friend she was talking to. She poured milk all over the tablecloth before she even noticed. She was a bit cross with him. But he told me when she came to give him his goodnight kiss he'd say to her, *Closer, closer* and she'd put her face so close their noses were touching. So, I know he really loves her.

And now we also have Iwi, who toddles round after us or sometimes just does things of his very own like spinning the wheel of the upturned pushchair or running to the back-garden tap to pretend to turn it on and grinning at us. Dad doesn't like us to leave the tap running. We must turn it off if we've used it. Just as we must put back his little nail scissors on the top of his tallboy next to his wooden hanky box with the little plaque on it. He doesn't mind if we use the nail scissors. He just likes them to be put back where they're supposed to be. Mum says, *He likes to be orderly.*

Our house is large and friendly, and looking in front of it towards the street there is a lawn big enough to play tennis and cricket on, and on the left-hand side, on the side next to the Harts, a stand of natives — a tōtara, a rimu, a kauri and a kōwhai — beside the honeysuckle hedge, and on the other a cracked path and the driveway and a lower hedge to the other neighbour, who we hardly ever see, and beyond them the Normans, our friends, Dr Jim in his brown suede shoes with doctor's rubber soles who was there when Mum gave birth to Iwi, his wife Betty with her jewellery, lipstick and bright red fingernails, and their fair-haired children Anthony and Sue. When Dr Jim walks, he slides past like a hovercraft over the shiny hospital floors and the nurses don't know he's coming. That's why his shoes are called *Hush Puppies*. He calls me *Janet Panet*.

Behind the house is the garage, then a space, then our washhouse-cum-tool shed with wooden slat gates and a fence on either side, and behind them is the orchard where the fruit trees are — an enormous plum tree that is lovely to climb, a Golden Queen, apple trees, a quince tree, some ordinary peach trees and a walnut tree — with a great high lawsoniana tree hedge all along the back that stops at the honeysuckle hedge that comes right up from the front, with patches of small lawsoniana underneath it.

Behind the huge apple tree there's a disused henhouse that we turn into a hut and wallpaper with the leftover green-white bobbly-surfaced wallpaper from doing up the boys' room, an asparagus bed, a vegetable garden and, at one side between the washhouse and the garage, a sandpit under an ordinary peach tree, one of whose branches comes out and goes slightly up.

I turn the branch into a horse and call it Brownie. I make it a saddle out of felt and some stirrups out of bind-a-twine I always get tangled up in, as well as a bridle and reins. I use Dad's little wooden box to jump up from, reminding myself to put it back in the workshop afterwards, or I just heave myself up, over the branch, into the saddle and ride and ride, talking and singing to Brownie and patting the branch to encourage it. Occasionally I glance backwards to see my mother waving from where she's cooking by the kitchen window, and I wave back. Underneath me is the sandpit and next to that is the asparagus bed.

And though he didn't mean to, that's where one Guy Fawkes night Iwi set off Pete's whole box of fireworks all at once with a sparkler. A rocket shot off between Mum's legs as she was coming in through the orchard gate. Jumping Jacks and Golden Rains started firing off into the asparagus, and Catherine Wheels whirled on the grass. Pete had saved up his pocket money for weeks to buy it all. At least one or two Golden Rains were left which we did manage to see shooting off their sparks. Pete and Dad had already nailed them to a fence post near where the guy was waiting on the bonfire to be burned.

All day in the hot sun we'd trudge around Morrinsville, pulling along our stuffed guy. He wore a boiler suit and was full of the hay we'd got from Harold's hay shed and was wearing one of Dad's old worn jackets on top of that. Kids trailed their guys behind them, and we shouted *Penny for the guy* as we went. I knew Guy Fawkes had tried to blow up the Houses of Parliament. But they'd caught him and put him on a bonfire to burn. Poor guy.

Sometimes, the orchard is full of long grass and the boys and I play hide-and-seek in it, burrowing our way along and making a furrow to lie in that hides you from view, and you lie face to face with the thin stalks and see grasshoppers and maybe an ant or a daddy-long-legs making its steady way up a stalk, and above all that the big blue space of the sky with a fluffy cloud or two, your heart beating wildly, waiting for shrieks and yells and *I've found her! It's my turn to hide now! You count to twenty! One . . . two . . .*

And sometimes we have sheep in the orchard to keep the grass down. I name what I decide are Pete's and my sheep Huff and Muff, which sound to me good woolly names, but Ian names the third one Joey which doesn't fit and is made worse because some of our mother Joan's friends sometimes call her Joey, and though she has wavy, sort of fluffy hair, she's nothing like a sheep.

The cry goes up, *The sheep are out! The sheep are out!* and if it is on the weekend and he is home we hear Dad call from deep in the workshop side of the washhouse, *Who left the gate open?* If not we all run up the driveway or the cracked path or round the side and over the lawn past the stand of native trees, go through the hole in the fence (the excuse to Dad being we must, to be able to catch the sheep) and into Alexandra Avenue, the double As and many syllables being lovely to say in your head when you have to write down your address — *twenty-one alexandra avenue.* Joan comes too, still holding and now waving a tea towel because she's running in that funny flip-flop way mothers run, her legs almost tripping her up. We decide quickly who'll go to the right, who to the left, split up and race off up or down Alexandra Avenue to try to find and round up the sheep and herd them home.

Peppy and Salty are no help. You can catch sight of Salty slicking down her black-and-white fur in the sun on the drawing-room windowsill next to the antique that Nanny, Mum's mother, gave us, with its crystal chandeliers that make rainbows in the sunlight. I make them tinkle against each other after I've tried to play the piano a bit from Pete's music notes. I can read them because I'm learning to play the recorder and Pete has shown me where Middle C is. Peppy has flopped her golden-brown sausage-dog body down under the snowball tree at the left-hand side of the house where she lies sleeping on the scattered white petals. She wakes up and runs excitedly round the front lawn, barking at nobody.

There is a strange atmosphere when one day a van arrives and parks in the back yard and a man in white overalls gets Huff (or is it Muff? We know it can't be Joey as he's smaller) from the orchard and walks the sheep to the van, its forelegs lifted up like hands between his legs. Joan makes us come inside. We aren't allowed to look out the kitchen window either. She tells us the man has come to take away one of the sheep and she won't let us watch. But we guess. He's come to kill one of the sheep, hasn't he? After that, when we get new sheep to keep down the grass in the orchard, I don't give them names. They're just *the sheep*.

2.

You try not to walk on the cracks on the concrete path that leads up past the flowerbed to the gate under the spreading oak tree. You might go before breakfast carrying the hand crate to collect the milk bottles, sometimes in the frosty winters with the cream having risen out above the milk under the silver bottle top, the cream itself in the half-pint bottle with the red foil top. Or you might go up in the early evening to put the bottles out for Mum, the milk tokens all clinking together in the bottom of one bottle and perhaps a note from Mum rolled into the top for the milkman.

If it is just starting to get dark, you'll race back down the path, leaping over the cracks, and bound up the wide, grey-painted wooden steps of the front porch, hoping the door hasn't swung to and locked you out. Then you'd have to quickly run back down and onto the path and round again to the back yard and up the back steps and in. And you mustn't forget then to shut the back door on the closed-in porch, where the painted wooden boxes for the firewood and the folded-up newspapers are, and where the apples are kept over winter at the entrance to the added-on boys' room that leads off it. And do all of this before the bogeyman can get in after you.

Or you might go to the gate and stand under the oak tree, fingering a picked-up acorn with its little hat or playing with one of its leaves, just to watch the buses. Our house is opposite the main entrance to Morrinsville College, which goes right up to the left to the corner and right down to the right till the driveway to Morrinsville Intermediate School at that side of the college facing the ballet studio behind Mrs Murdoch's house. All the buses taking the country kids home come down Alexandra Avenue and park opposite our gate. We sit on Pete's trolley or stand, an arm draped around the wooden gatepost (the gate was taken down early on), and looking directly ahead underneath the bus we watch the queues of feet come up pair by pair and left foot right foot lift into the air and disappear.

You must be careful not to get trapped by the funny man — he comes on the bicycle with its triangular plate covered in advertising and in front of that his wicker basket of leaflets which he delivers to all the letterboxes. He locks us in by the gatepost by turning his front wheel. He is dark-haired and red-cheeked and has stubble and a funny look in his eyes. Joan says not to be frightened; he is a bit odd; he isn't quite all there; we should feel sorry for him but be a bit careful. So, if the funny man is suddenly there, leering at you, you get a fright, wriggle out past his bike and race back down the cracked path and inside, not caring even if you step on the cracks. The name of the hot thing inside you is *fear* and you see the word panting out of you in letter puffs all grey and smoky **f . . . e . . . a . . . r . . .** and they're coming out of **YOU!**

Not a noticeably big boy, in fact a small boy, David, who lives up somewhere around the corner at the top of Alexandra Avenue, calls me over to the hole in the fence (our fence is large poles and buttresses of a creamy-painted wood with a kind of netting strung in between them) and says, *If you weren't fat and if you didn't have a cut lip, you'd be quite pretty.* I am devastated. I haven't weighed up my chances in the beauty stakes yet, though I do want to have a long blonde ponytail like Sue Norman's, and I know I can't. Mine is dark hair and my mother's friend Phillida cuts it for me and says short hair suits me so well.

But David is right. I am a roundish person who must look over her tummy to see her toes, and I've been born with a cut on my lip. Not a real harelip. My mother explains when I am old enough to understand that a harelip comes with a cleft palate that makes it difficult for the person to speak clearly — my palate isn't cleft, and my speech is clear, and I really like being asked to read aloud in class.

But at six months old I was weaned and apparently went with Joan to Christchurch where the surgeon stitched my lip together. *And how did you feel about me when I came out of your tummy? Didn't you like me?* I ask my mother when I am eight. *I loved you even more, darling,* Joan says. About my body and not being able to see my feet she says, *You're in proportion, that's what counts. And anyway, it's much more important what's on the inside than what is on the outside.* I try to believe her, but David's words go round and round in my head. Though more faintly.

My mother arranges for me to have ballet lessons at Mrs Murdoch's studio, newly built on the slight rise going down Alexandra Avenue before you get to the actual slope that leads to where the avenue makes a T crossing with the extension of Thames Street, the main street that goes right through Morrinsville from the stock yards to the football fields, before the road winds down over the bridge towards Tatuanui and Te Aroha.

The studio is behind the Murdochs' house, and with a troupe of little girls I learn the basic foot positions, which probably makes worse 'the Kemp walk' I already have, placing my feet outwards, as my father does — I walk like a duck, though possibly this is to counteract the fact, discovered years later, of my being bow-legged, though I can't tell because when I stand in front of the mirror there is no gap between them. However, if I stand with feet straight, immediately I look, as the boys do — well, Iwi does, at least — like a cowboy who's just stepped off a horse.

Mrs Murdoch is preparing us to take part in the Christmas recital to be held in the Morrinsville picture theatre, which has a stage. We are streams of little fairies in our ballet shoes with their ribbons laced up your leg and round your ankle and their soft pink leather cleverly gathered under the rounded toe and stitched to the smaller-shaped sole that doesn't stick out when you look from on top. Following various patterns, whose sequence I can never quite remember, we run in our traversing streams over the glistening wooden and talcum-powdered floor of the studio to a position the fairy leading our little stream knows. Then we lift our arms and do our foot positions and curtsy and bow. Then we run around in our streams again. I watch the girl in front and try to copy what she does.

On the big night, the Sugar Plum Fairy, the tiniest and daintiest little girl who goes to the other primary school in Morrinsville, so I don't know her, dances and dances all by herself, doing *petits jetés* and leaps and bounds, dressed in a pink tutu and ballet shoes, her hair done up at the back of her head with a sparkling band wound round it and with makeup on her face. I am bewildered. Where has she sprung from? From our little chorus line? From the wings? Why didn't we know she existed?

At the end of her performance, she bows and curtsies,

scraping from the waist low to the stage where she stands in the footlights right at the front, her feet in third position. Mothers and fathers and sisters and brothers throw bouquet after bouquet and posy after posy up onto the stage for her — so many that they are collected, along with numerous boxes of chocolates, into two large wicker washing baskets by Mrs Murdoch's helper. They are all for her.

I long for just one box of Cadbury's Roses to share with Pete and Iwi. I long for the light-footedness, the lights, the applause, the glitter and spangle of it all. I know I stand like a tennis player in the row of fairies, the wrong shape ever to be a ballerina. I imagine the Sugar Plum Fairy afterwards, after we've all gone home, muddling her name up in my head with that other character who put in his thumb and pulled out a plum. I see her sitting next to the baskets in a corner on the stage in her tutu with her legs and ballet shoes stuck out in front of her, taking out box after box, unwrapping and sticking her finger into and then eating chocolate after chocolate. Why does she have so many when the rest of us have none? Why doesn't Mrs Murdoch share them out, a box and a posy for *each* fairy? It is my first brush with stardom, and I am starstruck. The Sugar Plum Fairy is so much better than we are. She has eclipsed us all.

3.

Gradually Iwi grows from the baby I help Mum tuck into his various sleeping cloths, wrapping his arms in so they won't flail around in the bassinet or pram, into a toddler who inherits all our toys, the handmade wooden blocks painted all different colours, and little red indoor trolley on wheels that Dad made for Pete in the workshop on his lathe. Then the Meccano set, from which he and Pete and the Dive boys, when they visit, make huge cranes and hoists and trucks, trailers and front-end loaders, meticulously screwing in the little screws at the joints.

We are three and I am in the middle, both in age and because I am the only girl. But because of Joan, there are really *two* 'girls' in our family, for she is both my friend and my mother. Being two we almost balance up the males. Perhaps it would be nice to have a sister. But I don't.

All our parents' friends seem to have boys for children. Not only the Dives with three, the Mather cousins with three, the Bartons with three and the Haydon-Smiths with three, but there's also Bobby Judd, and he is an only child. And even lonelier than only, because of his callipers. He's the last polio victim in the southern hemisphere. His mother Jean rallies support for the Crippled Children's Society and to make sure children are inoculated against

The Kemp children — Janet, Peter and Ian (Iwi) —
at 21 Alexandra Avenue, Morrinsville, 1956. MORICE KEMP

polio in schools. We all line up to drink the pink medicine in little white cups. It's better than a tetanus injection and the TB injections, especially the booster, which really hurts and your arm aches for days afterwards.

Bobby Judd is very quick at taking his callipers on or off — each has two silver sticks to keep his legs straight, with black leather pads and buckles here and there. He is a bit jerky when he walks, but he's a champion swimmer with hundreds of ribbons and a beautiful style. Jean Judd is his coach. She spends hours and hours at the Morrinsville swimming pool training Bobby. Sometimes we call it the frog pond as it has greenish-coloured water and someone once saw a frog leap out of it.

At home Bobby has a bunk bedroom off the dining room. He slips his callipers off and slides along the carpet and leads Pete and me along to the hot cupboard. The parents are all in the living room, talking. They can talk and talk and talk all afternoon, having tea, eating cakes and pikelets, and laughing and later having little sherries. They never play. *Let's hide in here,* Bobby says, and we follow him in. He lets the bottom door we enter through close after us. *Now let's play mothers and fathers,* he says. *I'll be the father and Janet you can be the mother. Who'll I be?* Pete asks. *You can be our son.*

It is getting warm in the hot cupboard with the door shut. I say, *It's too hot in here. Then let's take our clothes off!* says Bobby. *No, open the door, open the door!* I say, getting upset and feeling shut in. We can't. It's one of those latch cupboard doors you put your finger into and press down, and that can only be opened from the outside. I panic and shout and bang on the door, and the parents hear us and come running and open it and let us out.

Bobby puts his callipers back on and Jean Judd takes the boys outside to go to see the piglets. I go into the living room and play with Iwi in his pushchair and wheel him round the Judds' house. When we go home, the dark is starting to fall over the farm paddocks and the cows stand quietly together after milking. Now and then, one looks up at the sound of our car. I watch the sunset colours come and the shapes of the clouds move and change. They hang spread out just above the skyline of the farms.

On the way back, Mum and Dad talk about the daughter who lives in a house on the first farm up Hangawera Road who has already cooked a Sunday dinner for the whole family. A roast dinner, with lamb and mint sauce as well as roast potatoes, pumpkin, green peas and Yorkshire pudding. All by herself. And set the table. She too is nine. Wouldn't I like to be able to do that too? For all of us? I certainly would not. I can't see myself having all the different pots and pans of things ready at the same time. Not to mention the plates hot and brought from the oven in oven cloths.

I feel resentful. I can't do that. I would rather watch the patterns and colours change in the sky. I would rather pretend I'm riding one of the clouds and dipping in and out where the blue is turning to pink. I can still help Mum. I always set the table and put the napkin rings with their initials next to the right person's plate, on the left-hand-side of their cutlery on their bread-and-butter plate, even though they might say J.C.K., as in my case — my great-grandmother's initials and not quite mine. And I can make pikelets. Though not quite by myself.

Sometimes when Dad arrives home from work and sits in the armchair by the fireplace in the dining room, having a little sherry and reading the newspaper while Mum cooks the dinner in the adjoining kitchen, I brush and plait his wavy black hair. He loves it and sort of purrs with delight and doesn't even mind when I put little ribbons on the end of the plaits and show him himself in the mirror.

But one day the boys and I are playing with Dad in the drawing room — a sort of rough and tumble — and we are all giggling and having fun. And he tickles us, and we laugh, but then I can't escape the tickling and I start to cry and cry. I am such a flood when it comes to tears. Dad says to Mum, *I give up. You'll have to bring her up. I can't cope.* What I hate most of all, though, is when he sometimes calls us brats, especially when we have to go on a Sunday drive sitting all three on the back seat of the car. Brats! What a terrible word. We are not brats. We are three lovely children, his own and Mum's.

The boy I like is the other doctor's second son, Christopher D'Arcy. He wears a light-brown corduroy jacket to primary school, and my friends and I find it lying at the side of the playing field, so they dare me to kiss it. I pick up the jacket and kiss it, and then we all run away laughing and go and hide behind the shelter shed.

Sitting in his father's runabout in the garage at the D'Arcys' place on Guy Fawkes night, when we climb up there over the trailer tyres having first, as Pete always afterwards teases me, fallen together into the ditch, Chrissy D'Arcy and I declare ourselves. *What do you want to be when you grow up? A farmer. And what do you want to be? A farmer's wife.* At this most moment of moments, both our elder brothers whoop and shriek and jump up the trailer tyres and laugh and point at us in the boat. *Chrissy and Janny! Chrissy and Janny!* they taunt.

But brothers cannot stop love. Chrissy and I know we belong. Besides adoring Chrissy and his corduroy jacket, I adore his name *D'Arcy* with its strange two capital letters with the apostrophe between them at the beginning, and the silent bump when your voice goes from the *D* to the *A*, as if you're going over a bump. Well, Jane Austen, here I come!

4.

To get to Morrinsville Primary School you turn left outside our front gate and walk up Alexandra Avenue rather than down, the way Pete scooted me to kindy. You go past the Harts' stucco fence and if no one is around, and you're feeling really naughty, you give the Harts' wooden letterbox a little push and it crashes down onto the grass on the other side. The Harts' house is way back behind their front lawn, and on the other side of the honeysuckle hedge behind it there are some sheds with their outdoor lavatory. Sometimes we can smell it if the wind blows our way and we are climbing in the honeysuckle.

The Hart children aren't as nice as the Normans, and Mr Hart is short and fat and sweaty and wears a hat. You must always be sure he's not coming when you go past. Or that Mrs Hart isn't watching from the back door up the long straight concrete path that leads to the letterbox when you push it. Usually, Pete is the brave one who creeps along lower than the stucco and pushes it off and creeps back. But then we laugh and run away and maybe they hear us then.

Further on, past Willy Water Rat, our name for the little stream where we lie in the long grass and catch spiders in jars, and past the Red Cross building and near the top of the street, is Mrs Freeman's lawsoniana hedge. You run your hand along the side of it as you walk by, and if she hasn't just had it cut, it feels like soft green fur. You turn the corner to the left, and you are now in Lorne Street.

A few houses along is the brick one with a low brick wall by the pavement filled with flower beds of brightly coloured anemones whose petals shut at night. If you stick your finger in in the daytime, they also close around your finger. It's nice. Very feathery and light so you almost can't feel it. Like a monarch butterfly's wings when you're rescuing it or putting it back on a swan plant.

Next, you must get past the Throwstones' place. The Throwstones are a raggedy family of many little children who sometimes throw stones at you from their unsealed driveway, so you must run fast past their house, so you won't get hit. A bit further on there's Mr Gallagher's dairy, then a few streets join not quite at right angles. One street goes down to the convent school where my school friend Jill Dinniss has piano lessons from one of the nuns, and on the other one it's just straight ahead to Morrinsville Primary School with the jungle gyms at the bend of the road, and way over the playing fields to the right is David Street School which you can't see, you just know it's there. You turn to the left, cross the road, and go in through one of the fence gates or right up to the main gates of *our* primary school and you're there.

In the asphalt courtyard I once found a shilling in a puddle at playtime. Jill and I decided I would say Mum had given it to me to buy my lunch with. So, I did, though I did have the lunch Mum had made me. She would give me special things like a cube of cheese and some dates in those little compartments at the end of the plastic lunchbox past the sandwiches. She liked to give us brown bread (though Dad liked white better) because she wanted us to be healthy. We would have Vegemite and lettuce sandwiches, or tomato and Chesdale cheese. I felt sorry for Joyce in my class who had just jam sandwiches and no proper plastic lunchbox with compartments. Joyce had blobs on her legs like the blobs the jam made on her lunch paper.

Jill and I had decided to help Joyce because she must be poor and went to sit beside her and make friends. We found out she was the eldest, and that she had to help her mother with the housework a lot and babysit the little kids. We knew there were at least one or two skinny, very white-skinned brothers, which meant they never had holidays at the beach, and others with running noses who were in the Primers.

We once went round to her house in the gully just before the overhead railway bridge to see if we could play with her. Joyce's mother came out onto the porch in a grubby dress and carrying a baby, with a toddler running behind her crying. We abandoned Joyce then, even though we imagined her inside doing piles and piles of dirty dishes by herself. It was all too sad and sorry. And her mother had looked so ferocious, fat and grumpy that we were frightened.

How the shilling came to be on our mantelpiece over the fireplace in the dining room that night, I don't know. I remember I had to wait for Dad to come home from work when it would be discussed. That was awful. The whole afternoon and evening were awful. As awful as the fact that I'd told a lie. I was lucky I wasn't a Haydon-Smith. The Haydon-Smith boys would have been taken into the washhouse and their father would have put mustard on their tongues. And if there was no mustard, then soap. You know what the taste of soap's like from when you accidently eat some that's got stuck on your flannel — you spit it out.

Dad and Mum stood there, way up by the shilling on the mantelpiece, and Dad made a speech about the truth which Mum agreed with, and I did too and said I was deeply sorry. Then I had to take it back to school the next day and give it to Mrs Brown, the Head of the Primers, because it was in the courtyard between the Standards and the Primers blocks though nearer the Primers that I'd found it. I had to tell her I'd told a lie and that the shilling wasn't mine and that someone must have dropped it and to please give it back.

Another awful thing happened once in the honeysuckle hedge where we were all climbing and tumbling on the flat top part where you could lie back, looking up at the sky, and not fall off. Beverly, our babysitter, was with us. It was a hot day and she made us take off all our clothes, then lie on top of her. I didn't want to, but she made us. She was lying face up with fluffy dark hair between her legs, and breasts showing, and you had to lie on all of that. Just for a minute. I was so glad when we all could put our clothes on and climb down. We told Mum, and although we'd once had a lovely ride on a cow in the paddock behind Beverly's family's house we didn't have Beverly ever again as a babysitter.

Sometimes, if we cleverly first ask Dad, who says *Go and ask your mother* and then we ask Mum and she says *Yes*, we go to the Saturday afternoon matinee in the Morrinsville Picture House. We see lots of Laurel and Hardy films — I like Laurel best, because he can pull such a sad face you feel really sorry for him. As you do for the child who suddenly drops their packet of Jaffas, those chocolate and orange-coated sweets in a cardboard packet . . . they go rolling down the sloping floorboards of the picture house and the cry goes up, *Someone's dropped their Jaffas, someone's dropped their Jaffas!* Hardy would have loved it, thinking it must be Laurel. And we see Charlton Heston in *Ben-Hur*, driving the chariot with four horses thundering ahead of him and winning the race. Breathtaking. We come home exhilarated and exhausted.

In winter, if there's ice in the puddles up the driveway, we crack them after pretending to skate two inches on them. I've never seen snow. And all the Christmas cards full of robins, which I've never seen either, and Christmas trees that hold their arms up, are unlike ours, which are lawsonianas with their arms hanging down. We deck them with blobs of cotton wool, pretending it is snow, and hang all the decorations from the box — little coloured balls on coloured threads, bits of tinsel, stars and spangled things — onto the branches, putting a star at the very top. We hang three long socks from the dining-room mantelpiece over the fireplace for Santa to put things into when he comes down the chimney. No fire in the grate, as it's summertime for us.

5.

It's the end of the school year. Mr Telfer, our headmaster, is leaving. He often calls me out of my Standard 4 class with Mr Dickey to walk round the playground, ringing the big brass bell to signify playtime or lunchtime. It's because he thinks it doesn't matter if I skip a few minutes of class. Janet Hamill and I are each chosen to present Mr Telfer with his thank you presents from the school and the staff. There's even a write-up about it and a picture of us all in the *Morrinsville Star*. It's so funny Janet chose to hold the largest present, as she's much smaller than me. I'm wearing one of the two nice cotton dresses with the little white collar that Mum bought for me.

In the holidays we go to a bach at Whangamatā. Once you've crossed the very flat Hauraki Plains facing towards Te Aroha and have left Thames on the corner of the Coromandel coast, it's a long dusty drive on a gravel road over the hills to the sea. I get carsick, so now and then Dad must stop the car for me. He tells me to watch the horizon of the road over his shoulder. Another thing I do is to play my ukulele, and we sing our way over the hills from the back seat. All the songs are there in a sort of rainbow I can see in my head — some to the right, or way over to the left like 'Rudolph, the Red-nosed Reindeer', because that's a Christmas song you sing at the end of the year, which in my mind is bottom left where a pot of gold might be. Whereas the summer holidays are on top — sort of over a long gap — then the New Year starts and some of the songs like 'Row, Row, Row Your Boat' begin. It makes us all happy and Mum says things like *Why don't you sing?* and she suggests a song.

At the bach there is sacking over the door to the outside loo. It is a bit stinky, and you have to sit over a hole on its wooden seat behind the sacking, but we do pour some white chemical stuff down into the hole and that covers the smell a bit. Very often the Dives are at Whangamatā too — in a big house with a veranda on the wide, long beach where the breakers come in. The smaller fibrolite bach we stay in is in the town, round past the wharf and in a bit.

Dad erects an old tent in the garden for the children to sleep in. We sometimes meet the Dives on the part of the beach nearest us, by the river leading out to sea. Jeremy, the middle one of the three Dive brothers, and I go in together, walking deeper and deeper and watching the water rise up my blue woollen bathing suit and his bare chest as we go further in, laughing. The mothers are lying sunbathing under sunhats on the beach, talking as usual.

Suddenly both Jer and I feel the sand under our feet give way and we realise we are in the channel and starting to be picked up by the current. I have just learned how to swim, but Jer hasn't, so I tell him to clutch onto me and I will save him. He does so with his arms round my neck, but the weight on my back makes me sink under the water, taking him with me, and we both swallow lots of water and then I struggle and swim up a bit and we come up again and breathe again, spluttering out the salt water, but it is no use.

Down we go again, and I start thinking we will be swept away, and we will drown. Then up we come again, and here comes Phillida, holding one wrist up in the air with her diamante watch on it, swimming one-armed out to us: she catches hold of us both and swims us back to shore, both of us still spitting out water and shivering a bit with the cold. They wrap towels round us and rub us and warm us. I say, *I thought I could save him, but I couldn't.* The mothers say, *It's all right, darlings, it's all right. You're both safe now.*

A few weeks later we have a goodbye to Whangamatā party at the Dives' bach because we must go back home and to school again. It is late January. We have had such fun and made so many sandcastles and moats and been out fishing in Harold's or in Morice's boats that I am sad. I creep along the little sandhills with all their tufts of toetoe here and there and that spiky dry sand-grass. I find a slate of leftover fibrolite and a chalky stone and write on the fibrolite *In memory of the Kemp & Dive families*, and the date, and half bury it in the sand. It looked like A. R. D. Fairburn's green-slate gravestone, half buried in the ground at Albany cemetery, I realise years later when I go there to seek it out. By then I know too that Phillida is Rex's wife Jocelyn's younger sister and that she knew him.

The best thing I've ever done is to win a bike. In our family you're allowed a bike when you're ten, and a watch when you're eleven. I am nine and three-quarters. So, I am nearly ten. Pete's eleven and a half and already has his big orange bike with a bar. Boys get on by swinging one leg over. I can't quite touch the pedals when he lets me have a go.

Bishop's bicycle shop is in Thames Street, which goes from the top end of Morrinsville to the other before the road goes on to Te Aroha. The red bicycle leans on its stand in the front right-hand window. It has a dark-red carrier and a silver bell. It is a girls' bike with space to slip your leg through so you can easily sit on the seat. Mr Bishop has propped a sign up against the front wheel: *FIRST PRIZE, Miss Morrinsville Junior Personality Competition. To be presented to the winner at the Sound Shell Variety Concert on New Year's Eve.*

I get an application form from Gallagher's dairy on the way home from school. Mum isn't sure if I should be allowed to enter. It seems not quite right for our family to enter competitions *of this nature.* I can hear Dad saying those words. If I ask him, he will say no, so I must get Mum on my side first. Many other girls are entering, though Jill, my friend, isn't allowed. But in the end Mum and Dad are both willing, and Mum helps me fill in the forms and send them off.

We're sure I won't come anywhere anyway, so I wear my best dress to the interview. It is light blue, sleeveless, with white flowers embossed on it in relief. It is princess-line which means it goes down in panels into an A and doesn't have a belt, so it is flattering. I am a bit plump. Mum made it for me on her sewing machine. It looks like the sky with some clouds on it. I wear white ankle socks and white peep-toe sandals with straps round the ankles. Mum lets me wear her white plastic poppit beads. You can un-pop them and make a necklace and a bracelet instead, and Mum tucks a folded white hanky round the bracelet, in case I need it.

I have learned all about the history of Morrinsville — about the Morrin Brothers who founded our town, the population, the name of the mayor, the fact that the sale yards support a hinterland of farmers with their heifers which they come into town every Friday to sell. This explains the long line of cars up our driveway when all the ladies come to see our mother while the fathers go to the sale yards. Sometimes it's difficult, as Phillida might have arrived first, so her car is at the top of the drive near our garage, where our boat *Joanne* (named after Mum) is parked; but she might need to leave before Jean or Marygold — and if so, all the ladies have to back their cars out and in again, in a different order. In between, they sit in the drawing room, having pikelets and tea and talking about the soul, that bit of you which is God. Phillida calls me *Darling* or *Janny darling* which my mother says too sometimes, and so does my father when he isn't cross.

All the girls who've entered the competition are sitting on wooden forms on both sides of the hall where we are to be judged. We must go in in pairs. We stand in front of a panel of judges including Mrs Gummer, who often wears very wide hats made of floral chiffony stuff — like flowery pavlovas. She's not wearing a hat today, though she does have a big silvery brooch pinned lower down from her shoulder to hold up a flap of her dress.

There is a window open high up on the wall behind them, with the light coming in, but the judges sit lower down behind a long trestle table spread with papers. One or two are men — I can't quite see their faces because of the shadow. We two stand in the light on the other side of the table, facing them. Mrs Gummer asks us if we go to the same school. *Yes, we do,* I say, trying to be helpful, for I think I've seen the girl before, but she immediately says, *No, we don't. I go to David Street and she goes to Morrinsville Primary.*

Already I've made a mistake. The girl is wearing quite ordinary clothes too, like school clothes, as if it's wrong then to wear your best dress. As if I'm trying to show off. But I'm not.

As you walk down our hallway in Alexandra Avenue you must be careful not to bump your head on our telephone which hangs there on the wall. It has a brown wooden case with the handset at one side. There are two silver bells on the case that clang against each other when the phone rings. The part that you talk into is Bakelite, like the stuff on Dad's car dashboard. When you've finished talking, you hang the handset onto its silvery bracket, first making sure you have untwisted the cord of brown cloth that encases the wires. We are on a party line. Our number is 909-D, and D is *long-short-short* in Morse code. I know about Morse code because Pete has to learn it for Cubs.

I can hear Mum talking on the phone. My bedroom with the wide windowsill with its rattan blind that you roll up to look out onto the nectarine tree garden is on the other side of the telephone hall wall. *Yes, yes, that's fine. Next Wednesday? Yes, she will be able to come then.* I rush out into the hall and look at her face. She's excited. She hugs me.

Later in my bedroom I go up to the long mirror and tell my reflection, *I'm in the finals!* I look back at myself from inside the mirror and I'm smiling.

I wear my best dress again as it is my *best* dress, and this is the finals, so I can't go backwards. Mum has washed and ironed it and the hanky, even though I haven't used the hanky. This time I go in alone and can sit on a chair to talk to the judges. Again, no one asks me about the Morrin brothers or the mayor or the population or the hinterland, or if we are in the Piako County in the Province of Waikato and whether those are the names of a tributary river and the major one.

I stand in front of the wardrobe mirror and the girl in the mirror moves, even though I don't. She says, *You've won! You've won the red bike.* Only she and I and the wardrobe mirror know. I open the wardrobe door and climb through over the shoes and past the winter clothes on their coat-hangers in the middle bit and come out the other wardrobe door, the one without a mirror.

Janet Hamill is also a finalist. In school, we are always first equal, or Janet is first and I am second, or I am first and Janet is second. You could say we are rivals, though it would be better to be her friend. We even have the same name. She is small and neat and has wavy light-brown hair parted in the middle with plaits and bows, and in winter wears hand-knitted, ribbed red cardigans. And she can think. Her father is the headmaster of a school near Hamilton. He has a very black moustache and thick eyebrows and black hair and looks much sterner even than my father. They live in one of the state houses over by the railway line, not in a bungalow of their own as we do.

All the finalists are lined up on the back of an articulated truck-trailer parked in the open space at the bus station next to the Morrinsville Public Library. All the mothers and fathers and brothers and sisters and people from the shops are standing below. There are twenty of us. A man at the far end of our trailer starts to speak to the crowd through a megaphone, asking each girl to take one step forward when her name is called.

I can see my tanned arm with the little golden hairs on it and then the folded-down white hanky in the poppit bracelet as I look along at the row of white socks and white or brown or red or black sandals. We make a nice straight line, which shifts one step forward for each girl. Then the man with the megaphone announces the third placegetter. That girl must step forward again. She will only get a book. Second place is Janet Hamill. She's to get a watch. Then the man says *And Miss Morrinsville Junior Nineteen-fifty-nine . . . Janet Mary* and my surname. I step forward, my heart bursting, my head pounding with pictures of the red bike on its stand in the shop window. I've won!

I catch sight of my mother standing below next to Jina, who runs the ladies' department at Gummers department store, and they are clapping and waving and smiling at me. Mrs Gummer walks along the row of girls and puts a huge red sash with gold lettering around me from one shoulder to my waist and pins it with a gold safety pin. She's wearing a billowing hat with a wide navy-blue band round the crown. As she leans over me to tie on the sash, I see she's got on her silvery brooch again, a sort of ferny spider.

She smells like ladies' talcum powder and her body seems planted like a tree right in front of me as she does up the safety pin. She's wearing navy-blue leather court shoes with white trimming and a pattern of tiny holes. When she walks away, I see she has such a big bottom it makes her chiffon dress skirt sway even further to and fro. Many years later in London I see a Scotsman in a kilt walk away down the street from a restaurant near Trafalgar Square. He too has a big bottom and his kilt sways as hers did. I can't help but watch the swing of the tartan pleats.

It's all over so quickly and now we are in a hydrangea-covered float — all the girls, some down each side, me sitting at the throne end, with Janet H on one side and the girl in third place on the other. We are driven down Thames Street in the New Year's Eve parade with all the other floats. I catch sight of my mother and Jina standing outside Gummers, throwing yellow HB pencils out to the crowd. Some land in our float. At least some of the finalists will get a pencil. One gets stuck in a hydrangea, then falls, I suppose, onto the road.

Janet is crying quietly. I don't think she ought to cry. She's going to get the watch. And she's already got a bike — it's aqua-blue and the handlebars go straight out rather than curving back as the ones on mine do. But, as we are enemies, I think I'd better not tell her not to cry, as she won't like it. The rest of us smile and wave at the crowd as we pass by. The street is lined on both sides. I'm still wearing my sky-blue dress with the red sash over it and my white cardigan. The sun is starting to set, and the streetlights are coming on.

The procession has finished, and Dad puts his sports jacket round my shoulders, as it is even cooler now. It is funny to wear a man's jacket. They are too big and much heavier than a cardigan. They have a different smell and all seem to be made by a man called Harris Tweed from Scotland. We are sitting in the front row on wooden forms watching the variety show on stage at the Sound Shell. A man signals us.

Dad stands by the steps beside the stage and helps me climb up. I wait at the top. The lights are so bright I can hardly see out, but I catch glimpses of the people of Morrinsville all sitting there, row upon row. Mrs Gummer is on the stage next to the compère at the microphone. They announce the name of the girl who came third and present her with a book. Janet comes up and is given the watch.

Then they say my name and I go forward into the bright lights. Mrs Gummer shakes my hand; a man wheels the red bike onto the stage, and everybody claps as Mrs Gummer gives me the bike to wheel off. It's *really* my bike now. Dad lifts it down the steps and we wheel it home together in the dark. We put it in the washhouse and tilt it to lean on its stand, next to Pete's bike. Later, Mrs Gummer tells my parents I won because I had such nice manners. My father is especially pleased, but I'm not very. It's only because of our parents that we've got manners, so we *must* have them. I could have told them so much about Morrinsville, but they never even asked.

6.

We are Anglicans. This means we belong to the Church of England. Mr Butt is our vicar. He is not that old and very friendly. We even have a sports club sometimes on Friday nights in the church hall where I once went to kindy. It's the old wooden church next to the new one with its separate bell tower. They're not real bells though. It's a tape recorder inside that makes the bell sound peal out. I go to Children's Church in St Matthew's every Sunday morning. In winter I wear my suit which is made of a nice tiny-stitched greenish tweed. It has a pleat or two over one knee and a jacket. Mum says it is well tailored in cut, and it suits me so well. And I don't look too fat in it. Billy, a boy I once liked and whose father has a telescope in a little wooden observatory at the end of their driveway, called out, *Hello Jumbo!* as I cycled past their place one day. I won't forget it.

Jill Dinniss is the organist, and I am assistant organist. This means I sit hidden on the top of the two wooden steps that lead up to the pulpit, just next to Jill on the organ seat, and when it's time for the *Venite* or the *Te Deum*, which are easy to play, we quickly swap places. I'm having piano lessons now, and like playing, though I'm not yet very good at it. Mr Butt just climbs up past me in his long black robes to preach the sermon, facing the other way. It's fun sitting there behind the swirl of black cloth, trying not to get caught in it.

I'm also in the choir and sing at Evensong. I don't have a very strong voice, but I can sing in tune and I'm a mezzo soprano. I must sing a solo, *The holly and the ivy / when they are both full grown* — and can sing it still. Once, Pete has to sing as one of the Three Kings. He is Balthasar. With two other boys all dressed up, they sing *We three Kings of Orient are / bearing gifts we traverse afar.* I like that *are* comes at the end, because it rhymes with *afar* even though you wouldn't say it like that but after *we.*

I am very devout and on the way to Children's Church I think about my deeds. I can still see me walking along past Mrs Murdoch's (the ballet studio is shut on Sundays), thinking about whether I have been good. And what it is to be good. I have even started to write something about God. It goes like this: *I know now that God is not a man up in the sky, counting our sins and our blessings.* And then I write on and on and on about how God is really us being kind and truthful to one another.

I like writing. I'm in Standard 4 now — the other one, for there are two, Mr Kilpatrick's one at the end of the corridor and Mr Dickey's in the middle. I'm in Mr Dickey's. He has dark hair and is nice. We go up to his desk individually to pronounce awfully long words from the list he has on a varnished card. Words like *magnificent* are easy but then there might be *pneumonia* and you must be careful not to pronounce the *p.* The interesting thing is you don't have to know what the words mean — just be able to say them.

Mr Dickey and Mr Kilpatrick are great friends. They are both tall and talk and smile and laugh with each other at playtime when they are on duty, maybe telling each other funny stories. Mr Kilpatrick is blond and walks as if he were on stilts and is very funny. My friend Jill is in his class and she tells us some of his jokes.

At school, when we're doing writing and it's time to hand our stories in, Mr Dickey always has to wait till I've finished, because it's got so long and complicated. So, he gives me another day. I know I'm really copying Enid Blyton and her *Famous Five* if it's an adventure. And I know that this is lazy reading. And that good reading is something else. I love *The Secret Garden*.

And though Mrs Brown did give me *Tales from Shakespeare* by Charles and Mary Lamb when I won the sweets competition in Primer 4 with my chocolate fudge, I don't read it. I keep wondering about the name — it's so long. *Shake–speare*. Nobody here is called that. I keep looking at the cover picture and the lettering and thinking I can't read this. It will be too difficult. *Oh child, what a pity*, says William from on high!

Mrs Brown takes the girls for Sewing in one of the prefabs. The boys go to Woodwork in another prefab with lathes and machines like Dad's in his workshop where they help him on Saturday mornings. Mrs Brown's fingernails are exceptionally clean and tidy and cut to a little point on each one. She takes tiny wee stitches with her needle and we learn to sew and to embroider our initials in red thread onto the white cap and the white apron each of us has made. Then we wear them in the Cooking class and the teacher can tell who's who.

Mr Pinfold, whom we know because he's our doctor's wife Betty Norman's nephew as well as a teacher, asks me to stay behind after school in Room 4 and play the recorder with him. All the wooden chairs except for ours have been put up on the desks and it looks as if we are in a jungle of varnished wood. He opens up the oblong recorder book called *Duets* and we unpack our recorders from their soft cases. Mine is a *Dolmestch Descant Recorder* made of brown plastic, but his is a wooden tenor recorder. It's much longer than mine and he has to fit the bits together before he can play it.

Then off we go! It is so lovely but so lonely sitting there playing piping music with him. The whole room is empty of the noise of children and filled now with the sounds of our music. I am happy but unhappy too. I'm not sure whether I am in love with Mr Pinfold. Once I took him some chocolate fudge on my bicycle to wish him a happy Christmas, but he wasn't there so I had to leave it on the doorstep.

But really, I'm not in love with Mr Pinfold, but with Mr Newell. He comes to 21 Alexandra Avenue sometimes and hangs his long coat and his hat on a hook on the back porch. While he is in the dining room having a cup of tea and talking to Mum and her friend Phillida, I write a little note in red pencil that says *I love you* and hide it in his coat pocket. I do love him, because he has soft lips and big, sad, slightly wet eyes, like a cow's, and as if he's just been crying because they are a bit red at the edges.

He guesses it must be me who left the note and doesn't

write back but does invite us all to come and see his paddock of daffodils in front of the farmhouse where he lives out at Tatuanui, quite near the Dives' place. So, one Sunday we go there and park in the drive and look. Thousands of golden daffodils are all over the front paddock. I've not yet heard of Wordsworth, but if I had I might have been puzzled about his name too, as I was with Shakespeare's. There is no Mrs Newell. Mr Newell says to Mum, *Maybe Janet would like to come and live here and keep house for me?* They all smile.

But I certainly would not. I'm a bit frightened they'll leave me there. And I don't like dusting and polishing the furniture anyway. I have to do that at home on Saturday mornings, as well as weed the rose bed, set the table every day and make my own bed. Because I'm the girl, I have my own room. I make sure the pink candlewick coverlet is pulled up properly and tucked under and then over the pillow. Even on the spare bed, though it has no sheets on it, so that they look like a pair.

Many years later, I write Mr Newell and one of my mother's friends a poem. I have seen their secret. I feel like Briony in Ian McEwan's *Atonement*. But it is the truth. And as lovers, they would have wanted me to celebrate them, especially now they are both long since in their graves.

A childhood secret

They were the first lovers I ever knew of
held in a house behind a paddock of daffodils
& I mustn't tell.

Wife-less, lifelong he loved her
& I'd see her empty car parked under trees
tartan rug & picnic basket from the back seat, gone.

They'd go in his car
to places he'd chosen in the bush, by a waterfall,
places less open

than his metal road where she first stopped
when he waved
& came from the cowshed to talk to her,

his eyes cupped against the light,
& with a hand more electric than a fence
touched her sun-browned arm.

One son, a cerebral husband and now he,
who held her fifty years,
all gone & she at eighty-one,

my 'other mother', here. How
he still holds her & the yellow flowers
she stands cradling.

Iwi has a bike too now, like us. But his is blue with handles that go sideways. They have re-done our road and Alexandra Avenue is pitted with chunks of metal and tarry stuff. He comes a cropper on the road, and we rush out to help. It's just awful as his knees are gashed deeply, and blood pours out. My own knees feel all the pain too. We get him to Dr Jim's, and he is stitched together again. But I know I can never be a nurse, as I'd thought I maybe could. A nurse must be helpful and not feel any pain herself or she can't help. I'll have to be something else, but I don't know what.

I am confirmed on 29 July 1962 by the Bishop of Waikato at St Matthew's Anglican Church. I have learned not only the Nicene Creed off by heart but also all the Statutes of the Church of England. I have a good memory and our vicar Mr Butt is most pleased. I love the rolling words coming out of my memory and out of my mouth, even if I don't quite understand all of them. Mum says the King James Version is written in exceptionally beautiful English, so that is the one I learn from. I'm wearing a white dress Mum has made for me and a lovely little gold necklace with a pearly cross from my father's sister Aunty Audrey in Christchurch. I expect a dove to descend and say, *This is my beloved daughter in whom I am well pleased.*

But no, I see only Mum and Dad sitting there with Jean Judd, and she is crying. I don't like that. It's like when Brown Owl left and our Tawny Owl cried. I leave Brownies after that, and perhaps I start to question literal belief after my confirmation. I hardly ever take communion again. I don't like the thought of eating Jesus's flesh and drinking his blood. I know it's symbolic, but I'd rather that love and being kind came and went between human beings as if it were ether. I think that's what Jesus really meant. Share my truth. Live my truth. Be my truth.

7.

Although I was born in Hamilton, I remember it only as the closest big town, because our family shifted to Morrinsville before I was one. Whether or not my father did cycle the 20 miles between the two before we moved, I've never found out, but when we drove the half-hour journey in the car, I used to ride with my poor father round every bend, thinking he could only have arrived in time to have to turn round and cycle back to get home before night. And what if he had a puncture? Would he have to spend the night in a haystack? Or curled up at the foot of a grove of eucalyptus, making a woven mat for himself out of their trails of bark?

Would my mother have given him dates and a cube of cheese in the small compartment next to the large one containing Vegemite and lettuce sandwiches, or his favourite, tomato, though they'd go soggy, or would he have taken honey or peanut butter ones, wrapped in greaseproof paper, in the little army tin with the leather flap that now sat on a shelf in his workshop near the lathe? Did children really skate up and down the swooping concrete sides of the Fairfield Bridge, as he said they did?

All I knew for certain about Hamilton and my father was that Dennis Wine & Spirit Merchants (and that meant Uncle Ron, though he wasn't a real uncle) had helped set Dad up in business in Morrinsville at Kemp Motors Ltd., situated a bit further down the road and on the opposite side from the Nottingham Castle Hotel, where my friend Marilyn and her sister Sue lived. Kemp Motors was on the last strip of shops, on the way to the stock yards, just out of town. And our mother became a particularly good driver, because Dad brought home so many different cars with D-plates, until they could afford to buy Mum a Morris Minor of her own.

Eventually our family would leave for Auckland — *for the Big Smoke*, as Gordon Spence, the New Zealand rep polo player and Morrinsville stock agent, used to say — for the sake of Dad's new job importing Simca cars, and for *the children's education.* But for us, in the meantime, Hamilton was the Little Smoke, home of Mooloo, the jersey cow, symbol and heart of the Waikato. Hamilton, too, had a magic for us besides that of its slow, deep, green, swirling river and the bridges across it and the heavy willows on its banks. It was somewhere to go to. It meant Mum and me driving from Morrinsville to the orthodontist during school time, with afternoon tea at Normie's, on the other side of Hamilton Lake, afterwards.

My mouth full of goo, patiently I'd count the dentist's neatly shelved and catalogued manila boxes of moulded teeth on the wall opposite, making arpeggio leaps up all the eights, say, diagonally from the bottom left, or skipping over the sevens. The one-armed tray would swing towards my mouth and the dentist's enormous pink fingers would be in it before you could smell the stuff the nurse dunked in cotton wool then squeezed into a tiny ball for him to dab your teeth with, and I'd be eye-level with the bits of the buzzer's drill looming in comb rows on a creamy Bakelite tray. Then he'd put the rubber bands in, right in the back of your jaw, to keep tension on the braces. This feat I was supposed to mimic, every night, after brushing my teeth before bed, and probably explains why it later took me weeks to master the intricate manipulations of dental floss.

Normie's superbly polished red fingernails never broke, and her shiny lipstick never came off, not even when she ate a pikelet with strawberry jam and cream on top. From her sitting-room window, you could see right over the big brown duck pond of Hamilton Lake to the fun park with the enormous slide that my brothers and I were sometimes allowed to go on. Isn't it strange that your own and everyone else's mother is so much nicer to you when you are alone with them or when there's other mothers and afternoon tea? They bubble like they do at parties — which, if it was in Hamilton, meant we'd stay overnight at 'Uncle' Ron and 'Aunt' Josephine's, and could play table tennis until even after eleven in the rumpus room with their daughter Karen and her older brothers. They made Karen seem like an extra or an orphan Ron and Josephine must have adopted.

I used to think my parents, too, had found me on the steps of the house at Bains Avenue (not brains which, like tripe, we never ate, as Dad hated it) I'd seen in the photos, because I had dark hair and both my brothers were blond. There I am in a long white lace christening gown, crowned with black hair, in my mother's arms, her face looking down at me, so happy. She wears a big floppy hat and a winter coat, and her mother is standing next to her. Next to them are my grandparents and godparents, 'Uncle' Jackson and 'Aunty' Wendy, with their son Peter and my own brother Peter. So, I do really belong to them.

Best friends

for Morrin Madill Rout

Their mothers — Wendy and Joan — 'd be so thrilled
if they'd known their daughters 'd meet now
both 51 with reddened hair and plump

as the baby cheeks they knew better than them,
one out one in the door of Hamilton's
maternity ward the same year.

Best friends smiling in hats & gloves
carrying christened babies in the boom time —
Waikato fathers out of uniform

at the showgrounds for Jackson's herds, Morice's cars.
In the Diocesan Boarding School for Girls' cubicle,
a silver mirror & hairbrush

Wendy gave her boarding-school Rapunzel;
on Joan's daughter's wrist,
the snake bangle she never quite understood

from godmother — were Joan to die she'd be Peter Pan's
& come, an orphan, to live in Wendy's tree-house
to grow up. She'd have a sister.

They'll meet, Wendy's daughter with daughter, Joan's without,
see how they've spent their mothers' legacy since childhood —
one dead, one without memory, fairies now, both lost and found.

Besides the river, bridges, willows, the orthodontist and Uncle Ron's, Hamilton was the place Dad went to hospital and we nearly lost him, as Mum said. Dear Mum. You could see, she'd been crying and was brave because of us. There Dad lay with an enormous plaster cast round his belly, his pyjama top loose over it. He still had black hair then. *It was the size of an orange*, Mum said. *What was?*

The cyst in Dad's tummy. What is a cyst? Something that grows into a lump when there is something foreign inside. What was foreign inside Dad? A 1903 Christmas pudding sixpence.

Hamilton seemed always full of combine harvesters and Massey Ferguson tractors, which every Waikato farmer had. Big, gleaming, new red or yellow tractors and front-end loaders decked the streets near to the wine and spirit merchants, the corner dairies, the ladies' hat and glove shops, and the department stores like Milne & Choyce, where ladies in pearls and twin-sets sent invoices overhead in shuttles, on singing wires, that rocketed along to a little grilled office and were taken out and checked and the change given and then rocketed back, making loud *shlock shlock* sounds as the canister was released from the tube on its return to the wire basket and the shop assistant.

All the prize bulls, too, were on the outskirts of Hamilton, tethered through rings in their noses to long chains, plodding their oblongs of paddock or staring out into the rain. Bulls with little tufts of hair underneath them, three-quarters the way back, as opposed to cows with their swinging udders. This is what Gordon Spence meant by education.

And there were aeroplanes at places like Te Rapa, just outside Hamilton, where Mum's English friend Marygold's New Zealand husband Hugh used to go, dressed up with his wings on, in uniform, to mess. Strange words those Air Force words, and even stranger images. Marygold and Hugh had lived through the Blitz which is when bombs fell on

London, and he had been a squadron leader in the RAF. His uniform was blue to go with the sky, whereas our father's one was khaki because it hid him amidst the desert sands. He had fought against someone called Rommel there and had been a captain.

A great-uncle, a real one, Frederick William, who we knew as Unkie, was Popsie's — Dad's father's — brother. Unkie had been a doctor in the horse-and-buggy days of Eketāhuna. Now Aunt Elsie was dead and Unkie was alone, old, and sometimes came to stay with us. He had thin white hair, a hearing aid that squealed, wore suits at home and spent hours on his knees at his bedside, praying. He was the constant supplier of the best chocolate biscuits ever, dark chocolate, with layers of pink or white wafers within. He wanted to help send my elder brother Pete to boarding school in Hamilton. Because he was a boy and the eldest. Otherwise, Pete would have gone to the ordinary Morrinsville schools like my younger brother Ian and me, for our family was not that rich. *Help send* meant Unkie had most of the money.

One winter Dad decides to build a runabout in the garage. We already have *Joanne*, the boat we take to Lake Karapiro nearly every Sunday, either to go on a jaunt up the Waikato River, maybe fishing and collecting blackberries from the banks, or for Dad to watch a speed-boat regatta or to try aquaplaning and water skiing on the lake. I can't water ski, though Ian is very good at that, but I'm a good aquaplaner. It is wonderful following the boat, with Dad happy at the steering wheel, looking back to make sure you're still there, watching the wake of the boat divide in a furrow of water right up to you.

Now *Joanne* is parked at Kemp Motors near the top of Thames Street, so the middle of the garage is empty, and Dad can build the new boat there. Along the two sides and at the back is all the firewood we helped him stack after someone had delivered it to the end of the driveway. First Dad builds a frame in the middle on which the runabout can take shape. It's going to last all winter.

Lake water is colder than sea water. My favourite is Lake Tarawera which I dive into from the short jetty, first looking at the mountain opposite, with its buried Pink and White Terraces. It is such a plunge down into the deep, almost icy cold dark emerald green of the lake water. Jean Judd and Mum sit on the little grassy bank next to the boatshed, or they're up at the bach we're staying in, talking and laughing with a group of other mothers as we children come up the steep bush path from the lake, shivering a bit under our towels.

They help rub us dry, or tell us to do it briskly ourselves. Joan is smoking. I hate the smell and don't like going near her then. We all visit the Buried Village and feel sorry for the poor people who were scalded and burnt to death when the mountain erupted. You can see all their things charred and blackened.

One holiday we spend at Lake Rotorua, staying in a Ngongotahā bach. I know about Hinemoa and Tūtānekai and how she swam out to him on the island we can see from the lakeshore with just a pair of gourds as a float. It's quite a long way to swim. So, I don't try that, but swim and flip, float and splash around like a dolphin for hours on end. At last Mum calls me to come out. *You're waterlogged*, she says, looking up from her book.

In 1956, Joan's first ever love, Bill Barton, was posted to Rhodesia and Nyasaland to set up a teachers' training college there. Much earlier, she could have married him and gone with him, but she was a little timid about his great plan to go overseas. Bill married the heartier Marcia instead, who did accompany him. Years later, back in New Zealand and Bill now the headmaster of St Stephen's School for Maori Boys on the steep Pokeno hill, the Kemp family are invited to spend Christmas with them. Some boarders stay at the school over the holidays, and with them and the three Barton sons we play soccer in the big hall and go swimming in the waterhole in the bush, pushing huge floating logs to and fro, slipping and sliding off them as we try to clamber on them to dive off.

8.

The wooden double-storeyed turn-of-the-century Nottingham Castle Hotel with its turret still stands at the corner of Thames and Studholme Streets, Morrinsville, where instead of the traffic lights there is now a roundabout. It was formerly run by H. R. Hadley (Prop.) whose name was painted above the side entrance door, and I always used to wonder whether Mr Hadley, my friend Marilyn's father, wouldn't have preferred to have been called *His Royal Highness Hadley*, but that wouldn't work because there weren't enough aitches.

To my mind Marilyn and her younger sister Sue were so lucky to live in such a big, old wooden building and to have the turret to go up into, to eat chocolates and read love comics and to spy out onto the townsfolk below from three floors up in almost all directions. Sometimes I was invited to stay overnight, and with a good supply of chocolates and love comics the three of us piled into and later slept in a huge double bed in one of the non-booked rooms, often quite near the Hadleys' own rooms.

There, Mrs Hadley often still lay in bed in the afternoons, resplendent in a lace nightie and bed jacket, eating chocolates and reading the newspapers. Quite unlike my mother who would have been busy in the household, baking biscuits for Dad to have with his tea, or preparing jars of preserved fruit from all the apples, peaches and plums that we gathered for her in the orchard. Mrs Hadley smoked, too, and the ashtray was always full of cigarette ends and the room stank a bit.

Mr Hadley would be downstairs behind the bar, day and night talking to and serving the farmers who came in for a lager or a Dominion Bitters from the beer taps and who then bought a case of those huge brown bottles to take home with them, because the bar would have to be shut at 6 p.m. on the dot. The six o'clock swill they called it. Especially on Fridays, when the farmers had all been at the sale yards, leaning over the fences, pushing and prodding their cattle or herding their sheep from the trucks into the pens to be sold and carted away by someone else. They'd need a drink after all that. I would park my bicycle in one of the sheds around the back in the large carpark where the farmers parked their cars and trucks, so you had to be careful not to get run over by any of them, especially after six o'clock.

Marilyn was named after Marilyn Monroe; though Marilyn Hadley has dark not blonde hair, it is about the same length as the other Marilyn's and curled up a bit. I think Marilyn wants to be a hairdresser. I like her because she's so friendly and open, perhaps because she's used to being nice to all sorts of customers who come to the restaurant and hotel that doubles as her home.

I just love going with her and Sue to dinner and breakfast in the dining room. Next to your fork on the left is a huge thick starched white napkin, and there is even a rose or another flower in a vase on each table. And at breakfast you can even have bacon and eggs, something we never have at home, Mum thinking porridge with milk and brown sugar is a healthier start to our day. Some of the waitresses and cooks are Māori girls who live either in the smaller workers' rooms at the back of the hotel or perhaps out towards Ngarua on the Kereone Road, or on their marae up one of the other roads leading out of town. Morrinsville's not a big place, though it has a hinterland.

On the opposite corner of Thames Street to the hotel is the bookshop-cum-stationer's called Echlin's where Mum buys her books from Norm Woollams. Echlin's is quite hard to say and I wonder why it isn't spelled with a *k* in the middle. Inside you can buy everything — books, stationery (spelt with an *e*), birthday cards, newspapers — everything to do with the printed word and writing, like pens, pencils, rubbers, staplers, even white ink to delete your own mistakes with if you are writing with a fountain pen, which I can now do. And blotting paper.

Just up the street a bit from Echlin's is the ice-cream counter, where some of the older girls sit after school, on high stools, dangling their legs down to the rungs on the stools and licking their ice creams. They're wearing their fluffy cardigans backwards, so they button up the back with the sleeves pushed up to their elbows, and tight A-line skirts. Some of them even dare to wear eyebrow pencil and lipstick.

And opposite and a bit further up is Joe Tong the greengrocer's shop. Our mother calls every greengrocer Joe Tong, even though they have different names and not all of them are necessarily Chinese. And then to top it all off, before the other ice-cream parlour on the corner before you get to the Methodist church and opposite that our Anglican church just past the dairy in front of the Morrinsville bus station, there is Bishop's bicycle shop, where my red bike stood in the window before I won it.

I use it whenever I need to ride anywhere, including on Saturday afternoons to go down to the bottom of Alexandra Avenue and across to the tennis courts, where I park and lock it against the fence and go in to play a few games of tennis, which I just love. I'm quite a good player. I think I've inherited Dad's eye for the ball.

Gordon Spence, No. 1 for the Morrinsville polo team in cerise jerseys, white jodhpurs and riding boots, lives with his old mother Mrs S in a corrugated red-roofed bungalow up a driveway from the road surrounded by the few paddocks he owns to keep his horses and the stock he buys and sells as a stockbroker at the Morrinsville sale yards. The shed out the back behind the house is full of saddles, bridles, curry combs and brushes. It houses the chook feed and the sack of chipped seashells Mrs S sprinkles round the chook run so the eggs will have harder shells.

Gordon's girlfriend Jina Hart is the buyer for and runs

the Ladies section of Gummers department store. Jina and Joan once had a dress they shared — shirt-waisted, brown with orange blobs on it and a revere curved collar with piping — that I later inherited, chopped up and made an A-line skirt from, using the panels already cut on the bias. Wearing it made me feel like a mix of Jina and Joan, as if I too were on a striped canvas chair in front of the line of cars at a polo match, laughing and happy and handing round bacon and egg pie.

On Gayvite or her daughter Princess, a swift little dark pony on whose back Gordon shoots many goals and who has a much nicer temper than Gayvite, Gordon rides up in the middle of a chukka if his stick has broken or if he needs his whip, and Jina gets it from the back seat of her pale-green Hillman Minx, parked next to our car, her back seat a heap of spare saddles and riding equipment and Gordon's spare pairs of boots, another cerise jersey and a spare towel.

I am out the back, under the trees, with Kevin, Gordon's chief groom, and the polo ponies, doing what Kevin says — walking them steaming and snorting after their chukkas to cool them down; throwing the awkwardly stiff canvas covers on and doing up the buckle at the front; or after the game taking a string of horses to the taps to hose them down and scrape off the excess water from their shining coats.

Kevin is so sour and never smiles. But he does love horses. You can tell. Before the game we would have them quietly standing in the shade, and go round bandaging each leg around the fetlock, taking care to stand to the side when doing the back legs in case they kick. Kevin knows the order of horses for the chukkas and has them ready when Gordon comes riding in to dismount and hand over the reins, takes his helmet off and wipes the sweat off his face with his hairy forearm, cracks a joke, saying *eh?* at the end of it, puts his helmet on again and rides off back.

After the match, in the prize-giving tent, Sir Woolf Fisher, no longer perched on his leather and steel-pronged shooting stick with the seat that opens out like a figure of eight, but now folded up and used as a stick with a prod to lean on, and wearing suede shoes, a cravat, cavalry twill trousers and either a double-breasted blue reefer jacket with gold buttons or a tweedy sort of hacking jacket, hands out the big silver cups for the season, and Gordon or Tommy Mellors, the No. 4 for Morrinsville, will make a short thank you speech, and they might all line up outside the tent for a photograph that will appear in the *Morrinsville Star — local boys make good —* when they've won against Taupiri or even the Kihikihi team who are pretty good themselves.

Gordon once took me droving. I rode Illustrator, the big bay gelding, my favourite because he had such a long stride, so cantering was quite easy. We took him exercising at the Rec and you could lie into his back and it would be smooth and powerful. Though while droving, we just walked along on horseback behind the herd of cows for hours round the back roads, me wearing one of Gordon's old oilskins from the shed that was too big for me. I felt like an old cow cocky with the huge poplars swaying on either side in their apple-yellow colours or if there were no trees and just cows who would turn to look at us, chewing evenly with lick dripping from their mouths.

We didn't disturb them. We were droving which goes at a slow animal walking speed. Quite natural. Just like sailing, I found out later. Then you have time in between countries to leave the one you've left and to arrive in the one you're going to. When I first flew in aeroplanes, I necessarily had to speed it all up.

My friend Jill could play the 'Minute Waltz' in less than one minute before she was ten, and her father, Tara, cut her fingernails for her so that they shone like half-moons. I ask Jill if she would like to help exercise the horses one Saturday at the Rec, if Gordon says she can come. I know Jill is highly strung because when we play the Māori stick game she always blames me when one of us drops a stick, even if it isn't my fault. But I know it will make her even tighter strung if I point out the truth. So, I shut up.

I should have opened my mouth when Gordon put her on Gayvite. Illustrator is huge compared to Gayvite, who struts about like a pony in show business. We begin by trotting, but Jill hasn't yet learned to rise to the trot, and it is bumpy. She sloshes around in the saddle, maybe even kicking Gayvite accidently with her heels. Gayvite must feel a temperament like her own on her back, making her even more edgy, and before Gordon, Kevin or I can catch her, Gayvite takes off and bolts, with Jill like a little rabbit on her back. Gayvite does her tour of the Rec, comes back to where we all are and, knowing a branch of a tree is low just by Kevin's tackle, scrapes Jill off her back. Jill tumbles to the ground, and Gayvite treads on her foot, Jill says. But it isn't broken. I don't invite her again and even if I did she wouldn't come. It is all my fault, I know.

But Jill and I are still friends even after that. Because my father loves music and can play the piano by ear, we have all sorts of records he plays on the radiogram, maybe to learn the tunes — Benny Goodman, Glenn Miller and his golden trumpet, Fats Waller (those are on the old 78s), and singers with songs like 'I'm Beginning to See the Light' and his favourite 'Rhapsody in Blue'. And because Joan likes them, lots of light opera and operettas — *The White Horse Inn*, *High Society* with her favourites Grace Kelly and Bing Crosby. Whenever Mum says *Bing!* her eyes sparkle. Bing has a very velvety voice. And she has Rex Harrison and Julie Andrews in *My Fair Lady*. I can sing the whole of the LP by heart. Jill's family have it too.

So, Jill and I think we ought to perform it for the Intermediate Department. Eddie Ware lends us the top hat he sometimes wears as a magician. It springs open or shut if you thwack in on your thigh. Because Jill is daintier than me, we decide she can be Eliza and I'll be Henry Higgins. As well, I'm Freddy Eynsford-Hill, Higgins' friend who thinks that he can *do it!* and Eliza's father, Mr Doolittle, who sings 'I'm Gettin' Married in the Mornin''. I wear a man's jacket from the drama club dressing-up box, and Jill a pretty flower-girl dress. We are a hit. We sing the whole thing through from beginning to end, unaccompanied, on the Morrinsville College stage.

The very stage where Randall McDonald with his crimped, waved gingery hair that sprang out from his parting when he got angry used to take the whole school — the college kids as well as the Intermediate Department — once a week for singing. He got angry very often and used to have tantrums in front of us all on stage. You could not escape. You just had to sit there and listen. No one was scared. I could see our house through the huge floor-to-ceiling side windows of the hall and down through the college gardens. Then we would all be singing again. He was quite pleased when we eventually got it right. I think music teachers are always a bit excitable. It must be the music that does it.

9.

It's 1961. Unkie comes to stay again. Mum and Dad have taken up his offer to pay to send Pete to St Paul's Collegiate School in Hamilton. It has just opened, and because Peter is the eldest, and a boy, it's very important that he goes. I am desolate. I do not want to lose having Pete at home. It will break up our family. But it is a must. Pete is a bit scared too but tries to be brave about it all. After all, he is thirteen now.

A few weeks later, we all get dressed up, especially Pete in his new uniform with its St Paul's cap and tie, and Dad loads Pete's packed suitcase into the car for the trip to Hamilton and his new school. We are going too, to see where he's going to be living. After Pete has unpacked his suitcase into the locker next to his bed in his dormitory, we tour the school with all its long low buildings, its chapel, and its huge playing fields and tree-lined driveway. On Sundays, many families come to visit their sons, and from now on we'll all spread out our rugs and have a picnic together, sitting on the bank of the playing fields, often watching the boys at athletics or other sports.

My godparents' children, Morrin and Peter, live so far out in the country at Te Ākau, on gravel roads and up the longest drive in the world with both a mailbox with a red flag and giant milk cans at the gate, they have to go to boarding school in Hamilton too. Boarding school brings horror stories of cold showers on frosty winter mornings and Seniors making Juniors do dreadful things for them. Brothers are known as Major and Minor, and you have to wear striped blazers and longs in class, do prep in the tower full of desks, and make your bed neatly every morning. But I suppose because I can go safely home again to Morrinsville, other trappings of boarding school seem attractive to me: the tradition and the fuss, the mothers' sepulchral tones when they talk of *St Paul's*.

Pete wins lots of prizes at prize-giving at the end of his first year — and for years afterwards — and we are so proud of him. Though I must say he is a bit gruffer when he comes home for the holidays to stay with us. A bit more far away. As if he has been somewhere else and doesn't know how to come home again. I wonder where he is. But soon he and Iwi start playing teasing games or setting out the train set and playing for hours together and he is his old self again. They don't mind if I come and listen to the Junior Request Session in their room on Sunday mornings, when Mum and Dad like to sleep in.

Jill is very quick on the basketball court and competes with Bye Hotene, who lives in Waitoa, just past the Dives' place at Tatuanui, where the biggest casein factory in the southern hemisphere produces milk powder for babies. So sometimes Jill plays centre for Team A and sometimes

Bye does; though perhaps the teacher should separate them and put one in Team A and one in Team B.

I used to be a goal attack, which I liked because you could move over two-thirds of the court as well as into your goal circle, but sometimes now I'm told to play goalkeeper. Maybe because I'm relatively tall, like Maureen Kingi, the other great Māori girl player. She is much nicer and more friendly than Bye. I wouldn't like to cross Bye Hotene. She might slap me in the face. She did that once to Jill, who immediately slapped her back.

We still go once a week to a cooking and a sewing lesson, using the bigger kitchens out near the enormous playing fields behind Morrinsville College where Ian and I sometimes go in the weekends to fly our kites. I'm making a pair of flannelette winter pyjamas with flat fell seams. Annette Garnett, whose mother is a real seamstress and makes people's wedding gowns and ball dresses, has already taught her how to sew. I have made such a mess. I sewed my flat fell seam inside out, even though in itself it's an inside-out seam, and I have to unpick it completely and do it again. The material has all the little holes in it from the sewing-machine stitching I did. So, I must iron all the seams again to flatten that out and re-do the lot.

For years and years I get up at seven o'clock every morning, even in winter. Mum usually wakes me. Then I go into the cold drawing room and practise the piano for half an hour until half-past seven. I started the year after Pete did, so in the meantime I taught myself some of his easier pieces. Our teacher is Mr Cranna. But now Pete is at boarding school, so I go once a week on my own. Mr C calls me his star pupil and after each lesson puts up stars on a chart. I have just passed Grade 3 of the Royal Schools of Music, both Practical and Theory.

I can do arpeggios and scales and play 'Heimweh', which is German and means longing for home, very tenderly. It makes your heart feel painful, playing it. Also, some of Bach's 'Prelude', which is easier as there are no sharps or flats, and Handel's 'Largo', and I'm beginning at home by myself on the 'Moonlight Sonata', though it is quite hard to stretch your hand across the octaves. I know I am still years and miles away from the 'Minute Waltz'. But Mr C wants me to skip Grade 4 and go straight into Grade 5 next year. It is awful. I cannot do it — I know I can't.

I get on my bike leaning against his plum tree halfway down his driveway and start crying. The tears run all the way home. I tell Mum I never want to go to piano lessons again. It's too much and too fast and I can't. I take refuge at home at the piano. I sit there for hours, playing and playing and making it up as I go. I do big, long, deep dark chords and invent twinkling passages and go onto the black keys as if I knew all the scales. My eyes are shut. I go on for hours, and Joan never complains, nor even peeps through the glass door that leads to the hallway. But I know she is listening. She just loves music. And her father, our Buppa, still plays the organ in the Congregational church in Mount Eden.

If they have parties, I sometimes wake up and peep through that door made of wooden struts with squares of glass, so you get a good view. There are ladies in sparkling strapless frocks, smiling and holding their cocktails and laughing and talking. Dad is at the piano and everyone is saying, *Wonderful, Morrie, play another one.* Dad is smiling and expansive and has a cravat on. Some of the men lean on the piano, looking down, or Jina does, looking so appreciative that Dad can play. He has no notes; in fact, he's put the music rack back inside the piano and you just see its mahogany and lighter inlaid wood shining above his twinkling moving fingers. He plays by ear.

Every morning when I've finished my practice, I shut the piano lid and go to the window ledge where Salty often sits, just looking, and I tinkle the hanging crystals on Nanny's green antique. In the sun the dangling swinging crystals make rainbow patterns that dance into the dark drawing room — dark because it's panelled in wood, with a frieze up by the ceiling which goes right round the wallpapered room.

On Sunday nights in winter, we wheel in the trolley and sit around the fire, having boiled eggs and toast and Vegemite. The eggs are in little silvery egg cups with cut-out sides, and you must unhook your egg spoon from the egg-spoon stand that is like a carousel in the middle of the tea trolley. Dad likes to put salt on his boiled egg. Then he cuts his slice of toast into fingers and takes a bite from each, one after the other, so that it mixes in his mouth. So do we.

Dad also loves to slice a tomato and have it on his toast and sprinkle a bit of salt on it. But that is in summer. He especially likes the ones he has grown himself in the back garden. They really taste like tomatoes. His other favourite thing to eat is a Golden Queen peach. He'll sometimes pick one straight from the tree in the orchard and cut it into slices with his little silver pocketknife and share it with you. They are so juicy; the golden juice runs down your chin. He likes the Golden Queens much more than the other pink and green sort.

Just across from the plum tree and into the next section, they have built a new house. The people in it are Americans. Mr Bevel is a new teacher at the college. He wears big square glasses that keep falling down his nose. He has a Russian class in Hobbies. I learn *Volga Vodka* and *horoxo*, which means good, as well as *I do* or *don't speak and understand Russian*, and *goodbye*. It is difficult, as there is a whole new alphabet with that strange X in it. But then we sell the house.

10.

Gordon again says *Why are you going to live in the Big Smoke when all the education you need you can get from looking over the back fence?* Then he laughs. He means cows getting calves after bulls have been with them.

It is 1962, I am nearly thirteen. At Morrinsville College Intermediate Department I am joint dux with Janet H, and Mr Ware says one day I should go to university, for I have a high intelligence quotient. It is only because we did an IQ test with lots of language and geometry and other puzzles in it and I got the highest mark. There is still another year to go before we must move to Auckland, so I will begin Form 3 at Morrinsville College.

Don Clarke, *the Boot,* buys our house from my father. He comes round to talk to Dad. It is strange seeing him in our dining room in our chair and not on the footy field kicking a goal between the posts. His brother whose name is Ian, just like my brother's, has a cauliflower ear. If you get up close after a match you can really see it, once he has taken off his leather helmet that makes him look like a pilot. The men have short black pants and huge muscles in their legs, and footy boots with studs and thick woolly socks. I see them at Campbell Park on Saturdays when I play basketball there.

Don Clarke signs my red autograph book that Aunty Audrey gave me. She has written in it *Be good, sweet maid and let who can be clever . . .* and then something about *not dreaming dreams all day long.* Don Clarke just writes *Regards, Don Clarke.* I am thrilled. Though I prefer Pat Boone.

Mr Ware is at Phillida's house and is giving a magician's concert. He has a little white wooden fence and a tiny white house that he sets up in the big living room and does his tricks as if on the front lawn. Then he says, *Janet, you can pretend to come and fetch me and take me home.* But I don't want to. He is a bit soppy, I think. He is a wonderful teacher but I'm not in love with him. And it's all very sad, because his wife is crippled with a disease called multiple sclerosis and sits at home with Anne W in her cardigan who has to be grownup already, looking after her.

At Phillida's on Sundays, when we go there for lunch and the afternoon, I sing *Tammy's in love* into the microphone of Harold's reel-to-reel tape recorder, full of as much love for Pat Boone as I can make my voice sing. Phillida thinks it is wonderful and encourages me. I also read out a poem I've written. She tells me her sister Jocelyn was married to Rex the poet, but he sometimes loved other ladies too. And that this happens sometimes. She is my first 'other mother'. I adore her. She says I am a chrysalis from which one day a butterfly will emerge.

1962

—

1966

1.

Mum inherits some money from an old aunty who has died — it might be Aunty Pat or Aunty Elsie, two of Nanny's sisters. It is enough to buy our own bach. We look and look and find one on stilts at Whitianga, on Buffalo Beach Road. Across the road from our bach and on the sandhills leading to Buffalo Beach there are two trees hugging close together and two aloes, those big juicy, spiky plants. They flower only once in a hundred years. From the upstairs windows or the veranda you look out across the road over the aloes and over the sandhills to Mercury Bay and beyond that over the sea to the islands. Captain Cook came here once to observe the Transit of Venus, as it says on the monument on the headland at the other end of the beach across the river from the wharf.

I help Mum make red and white checked sheets and curtains for the bunk room — that's for us three children

— and blue ones for her and Dad's room, though in the end the boys help Dad put up the tent in the back yard and they sleep there on camp stretchers. Outside the tent we play tenniquoits.

We go to the bach every summer for six weeks. We just love it there. Dad goes back to Morrinsville every so often to check up on his work at Kemp Motors, but we stay on at the bach with Mum. Besides, there are not only the Dives over the hill at Simpson's Bay but also the Millers are nearby.

We all have boats, and the men go fishing together, or we go on picnics to Hahei or the Elephant's Leg and places you can only reach by boat. Iwi falls out of a tree climbing in the bush behind our bach and must wear his broken arm in a sling all summer, which means he can't go swimming. We give him one of Mum's knitting needles to poke down inside the plaster in case his arm feels itchy.

We go fishing way out in Mercury Bay by the Hole in the Wall, and on the way, we trawl for kahawai which we then cut into little pieces on the floorboards of *Joanne* and use on our hooks to catch snapper for our dinner. I love the crystal bowls of spray *Joanne* makes on either side as she pushes on through the sea, leaving behind a long silvery wake of water that turns over itself at both sides with a trail of white in the middle.

With the Dive boys we build huge sandcastles on the shore and watch as the tide comes in to take them. This year, the last before we move to Auckland, the Millers are staying just along the road from us on the right past the aloes and on the beach side among the sandhills. Mary Miller and I love singing together and playing our ukuleles. Together we write a song that we sing with American accents, *Dear Johnny this is my last letter* (making long *r* sounds), *dear Johnny I guess this is goodbye, oh darling won't you answer my last letter* . . . and how each day we wait for the postman for his letter, but none comes. It's very sad but we laugh a lot.

Marygold, Mary's mother, has just come back from her round-the-world trip. She won 'It's in the Bag' on the radio by answering all Selwyn Toogood's questions, and has been everywhere — in rickshaws in Hong Kong, looking at turtles on the Galapagos Islands, and she's been in Hawai'i, so she knows about muumuus, the colourful straight shift dresses without belts but with a white fringe round your knees, like the fringe around a sun umbrella.

Our mothers help us make a muumuu each on their sewing machines, and Mary and I enter the New Year's Whitianga Talent Quest. We are thirteen and a bit. Mary's not afraid, so I try not to be too. We must sing in the Sound Shell on New Year's Eve before a big public audience. The Mums are there, waving happily and wearing their muumuus too — they clap and clap after we've sung, and we come second! First prize goes to Bill & Boyd who become real singers after that. Our families are so proud of us both. Mary could even have gone in for the Miss Whitianga competition, but she tells me she wanted to meet a boy down on the beach, so she didn't. I'm sure she would have won it too, with her beautiful slim legs and bright personality.

Dad needs to start his new job in Pakuranga, but I must finish the year, so I go to stay with the Millers at Kiwitahi for the six weeks leading up to the Christmas holidays. There are four girls — Bridget (known as Squeak), Rosy, Mary and Cathy — plus James, who has a little outhouse behind Marygold and Hugh's white-stucco, green-roofed farmhouse. The Millers' farm has cattle and sheep on the further-away hills. We help Hugh feed out, which means standing on the back-trailer, shovelling ensilage onto the paddock, the cows hungrily following, while Hugh drives the tractor, cracking jokes all the way. There's also a horse, Jimmy, who I love riding. But as Jimmy has already taken the two small girls to school at Kiwitahi Primary and back during the day, he doesn't really want me to ride him in the late afternoon.

Mary and Cathy have a huge shared room next to James's cabin, and there's plenty of space for a bed for me too. Every morning after breakfast we catch the school bus for the long ride into Morrinsville. At last, it's *my* feet I could have seen getting off the bus from across the road, but we don't live in our house any longer. Don Clarke does.

2.

We've bought a new house! It's at 30 Waterloo Street, Howick, Auckland. Now Mum is in the same town as her parents, our Nanny and Buppa (because Ann Pemberton, the eldest of all the cousins, couldn't say 'Grandfather') and Mum's older sister Mary, who was once Mary Hooton. Their brother David Hooton, a physicist, is ten years younger again than Mum, and lives in Edinburgh with Margaret and their two daughters, Frith, who was born in Scotland and named after the girl in *The Snow Goose*, and Briggy, named Brighid as she was born in Germany. We all gather at the Pembertons' tall brown house — it looks like a doll's house — to celebrate Buppa and Nanny's golden wedding. It is 8 October 1963.

In our childhood we always drove up from the Waikato to stay with Nanny and Buppa in their big villa at 33 View Road, Mount Eden. We knew their address off by heart because of writing our thank you letters and putting it on the envelope at Christmas or after our birthdays. *Can we see the lights . . . can we see the lights . . .* we'd chant as soon as we got there, and Nanny or Buppa would say, *We'll have to wait till it's dark.* Then we'd climb on the couch under the big window in one corner of the kitchen and peer out down the valley at the twinkling, coloured lights of Auckland.

Or, getting up early in the morning before the parents, you'd go into the kitchen and there was Buppa already sitting at the table. *Would you like a cup of tea and a piece of bread and butter?* he'd ask. Then he'd butter the end of the loaf and, using the breadknife very carefully, he'd cut you the thinnest possible slice and fold it in half and give it to you. *There, a bread-and-butter sandwich.* Later, when the real breakfast was on the table, we'd all pour a sea of milk round each of our islands of porridge. Buppa then took the fan-shaped silver spoon and instead of sprinkling it, he bumped his holding wrist from underneath with his other hand and the white sugar spread very evenly all over the porridge island.

The other must-see was on the long way to Auckland — the car-on-the-pole. Suddenly you'd round a bend and there it was, and one of us would shout, *There's the car-on-the- pole!* It was in a paddock on the left going up and, on the right, coming back, sitting there on the top of a pole. An old vintage car. Dad knew what sort. He'd say *a Morris Minor* or *an Austin Prefect* or *an MG* without having to think — he just knew.

Buppa played the organ in the Congregational church which is huge and made of concrete and you only have to walk towards the mountain end of View Road and you're in it. There he sat, way up high, his white head visible over the top of a green velvet curtain on a brass rail. You could see his hands go up or down onto the various keyboards — two or three of them. At home in their drawing room, known also as the music room, he had both a piano and a little organ that you played by putting your knees together between two flaps of wood and pumping your feet up and down to fill the pipes with air while playing the notes with your hands on the keyboard. Later, after they moved to Howick, Buppa presented the organ to Bishop Selwyn's All Saints Church, where it sits to this day. The plaque reads *Donated by A. J. Hooton*. The gentlest grandfather in the world. I visit it on trips home and sit proudly on the seat.

Nanny would gather us in the sitting room and take out the leather-covered albums full of black-and-white photos. She'd lay them on her knees and spread them open onto ours, too, then explain who all the people were — Aunty Pat and Aunty Elsie, her other sisters (there were thirteen children altogether), and Uncle Zante, the poet (I don't know yet that he must have been named after a Greek island, nor do I yet know of Dante). I like Uncle Zante the most because I write poems too.

There's also Enoch Spragg and all the Spragg family sitting in wicker chairs or on the grass all over the lawn in front of their house, 'Warwick', in Mount Albert. They named it Warwick because they came from Warwickshire in England, Nanny said. Great-great-grandfather Enoch Spragg has lots of long fuzzy white hair and a huge beard, and the ladies wear long dresses. The Spraggs even have some bush in the Waitākeres called Spragg's Bush, which

Nanny says they *gave to the nation.* As Buppa's family did with Hooton Reserve at Albany.

Staying at the Pembertons' in the holidays was always great fun. They had discussions at the dinner table on all sorts of subjects. I loved it and tried to open my mouth but was a bit tentative about having an opinion on anything. At the same table, Aunty Mary, who was Head of Maths at Auckland Girls' Grammar School and was the top of New Zealand in Scholarship in her year, coached me in arithmetic so that my marks did improve. But she could also be fierce. If she was cross with one of the Pemberton children, she called, *Come into the little bathroom, John!* (or Ann, Judy, Roger or Helen, though rarely Helen, the youngest of all the cousins, as she was never disobedient). Aunty Mary would then give them a slap on each hand with her little leather strap with its red wooden handle.

The little bathroom under the stairs was tiny, too, and Aunty Mary very tall and big and grim-looking when she was cross. John, her elder son, was the leader of our little pack, so he hid her leather strap by burying it in the garden. He called himself *Tamber John Richard Pemberton* because he was a lion, he said. Judy he called *Catfish*, which she didn't like. I forget my name, and Roger's — John's gentle, dark-haired younger brother who had a streak of white hair like Indira Gandhi's, even when he was little. Hennie was too young to be in our pack and sat on the back doorstep, sucking her thumb and playing with her doll. Ann would be upstairs in her room, reading a book.

But Aunty Mary did organise activities for us all. We visited the Auckland War Memorial and Museum, way on top of a hill with a view out and over the harbour bridge, the sea and Rangitoto and Waiheke Islands, to see the giant war canoe and stand under a food store and go inside a meeting house.

By contrast, Uncle Dick was lively, playing the mouth organ or bouncing each child piggyback up the stairs to the bunk room singing *Rumpty-tiddly-umpty-pom* when we cousins came to stay at 31 Sale Street, their tall brown two-storied 'doll's house' in Howick. He was lieutenant colonel to Dad's Captain Kemp in the Sappers, and Morice was best man at Dick's wedding to Mary Helen Hooton, and so met her younger sister, our mother Joan, who was then serving in the Red Cross.

Our own Howick house at 30 Waterloo Street is down a steep driveway, on the left-hand side of a steep front lawn which Dad always mows on Saturday mornings. There's a carport rather than a garage, and my room looks out through a sash window onto a little square of bitumen just behind the carport to the next-door neighbour's hedge. Beyond that the section drops away into the little gully and there's a backway path on which you can take a shortcut that leads up to the Howick shops.

I plaster all the walls of my room with pictures of Pat Boone and Shirley Jones who sing together in the film *April*

Love. I can sing it, too, including the half-spoken refrain at the beginning. I see April — well, Shirley — as a real girl who must be seventeen. And is blonde. But I'm only fourteen. And dark. But it doesn't matter. I pretend I'm Shirley so that Pat will be singing to me. I'm quite soppy really. There is a man in a white shirt and black trousers, who must be a family friend, who sometimes visits us. I forget his name. He's tall and handsome. But he doesn't wear blue and white checked shirts like Pat. And he seems to like talking to me rather than singing.

Ian's room is next to mine on the left of the entrance door after you've come up the steps. The big living room is opposite my bedroom, and Mum's and Dad's bedroom leads off that. The kitchen opens onto the sunporch, so that when Mum's preparing dinner she can talk to Dad over the ledge above the sink while he's sitting on the divan.

One day Dad sits solemnly on the divan with me and explains to me what gang-rape is and how I must be careful not to go out alone at night in case there are gangs of boys who might follow me down the backway and want to lie on top of me one after another. I've never heard of gang-rape before. But it's a sign of trust that he wants to warn me about it, I think, even though it sounds awful and I'm not *quite* sure what it is. Though I know how babies are made, because in our sitting room in Morrinsville Mum once explained it to us, showing us with her hands how the part of the man went inside the woman to make a baby. We giggled at the thought. It looked so funny.

I'm outside on the front lawn, perhaps weeding the flower bed, when a cry goes up from the lady next door to the whole street, *President Kennedy's been shot in Dallas!*

It's a frightening moment. We are all stunned. We hear the news report on the radio when Dad gets home from work at six o'clock. I don't know much about America, though we did have that new neighbour in Morrinsville who taught Russian, and there are some American Field Scholars at my new school, Pakuranga College, where I've been put into 4 Academic A. Later I learn everyone in the world knows exactly where they were when they heard the news about Kennedy.

We stay only a year or two in Waterloo Street, then move to 7 Seymour Road, Mellons Bay. This is a brick and tile house with a small, level front and lower back garden, and internal garage and basement. Dad's war trunks are in the basement — the larger one is khaki like the uniforms and army blankets that lie in it until we take the blankets to the bach in Whitianga, and the smaller one is navy blue.

I carry all my dolls down the internal staircase in my arms and lie them on the uniforms and tuck a blanket under their chins. One of them — it used to be Mum's and before that it was Nanny's, so it really is old — has a face made of china and old lace on the collar around its neck. I've decided I'm too old now to play with dolls. And I don't need to have one sitting on the little chair which sits on the sunporch in Nanny and Buppa's house. The little chair has an inscription in Nanny's handwriting.

> *Grandpa's chair — (made for a child).*
> *This chair, which is 80 years old, was made by my grandfather Charles Spragg — with pieces of wood he picked up. The twisted bits are 'Supple-Jack' & the seat 'Rewa-rewa'. With the exception of the seat, which was shaped by hand, the wood is in its natural state — 1880 — Dorothy Hooton P.T.O. To be given to the youngest daughter of the youngest daughter.*

So, because our mother Joan Anne is younger than Aunty Mary, she will inherit the chair, and after that I will, as I'm the only daughter. Speaking of grandparents, Gran (Edith Louise) and Popsi (Alfred Geoffrey Kemp) must not be forgotten, although we know them far less well than Nanny (Dorothy) and Buppa (Arthur John Hooton) because they live in faraway Christchurch, where Dad's sister Aunty Audrey lives too. We write them thank you letters twice a year — at Christmas and on each of our birthdays. Sometimes we are not quite quick enough, and Aunty Audrey writes first: *I haven't yet received Janet's / Peter's / Ian's thank you letter.*

She is a maiden aunt and was in Japan during the war, helping the wounded soldiers before they came home. She fell in love with one of them but unfortunately they didn't marry. So instead she looked after her ageing parents at home, at 106 Glandovey Road, Fendalton, Christchurch. Alfred Geoffrey Kemp had worked in insurance in Westport, where my father Morice was born in 1905 before the family moved to Ōamaru, then Tīmaru, then finally Christchurch. Mum has some lacquered Japanese dishes that Audrey gave her and Morice, her only sibling.

Aunty Audrey's a great card sharp and plays Bridge with some neighbours. She also gives us her bamboo and ivory Mahjong set, with all the tiles intact and the wooden racks to line up your tiles in — though that game comes from China, not Japan. Eventually she needs to wear a wig, which sometimes slips a bit.

Audrey types up all of Dad's war letters on her typewriter and keeps them in a folder. He calls the Germans *Jerry* and has great respect for the soldiers who are just like his men. He and his team unearth the German minefields and lay the Allied ones in their place. On their days off they go to Cairo in a jeep, and sometimes Dad plays the piano and the men gather round and sing.

He tells us of *the belly-dancer who might have been your mother*, and — much later — on his eightieth birthday Marygold Miller hires a local Howick belly-dancer to come and dance at the little party for him at home. Mum chuckles. She knows him well. He likes his sherry every evening at six o'clock before dinner, and likes to sit with her, drinking sherry and eating a peanut or two from one of the wooden bowls he turned on his lathe in the

Morrinsville workshop next to the laundry and polished smooth and then varnished. He tells her about his day and she tells him about hers.

3.

We must wear a uniform to school — but unlike the Morrinsville Intermediate School's navy-blue gym frock in winter, the colours of Pakuranga College are bush-green and white. Much nicer. I stand there in my green and white uniform on the stage while the whole of the college sits in the assembly hall. I'm giving my speech about Thor Heyerdahl and his Kon-Tiki expedition in the annual speech competition.

You must control any anxiety and just remember to speak on, using your carefully written notes, and look up now and then at the audience. I've never been to elocution classes, but I still win. The judges say it's because I articulate so well, and the speech was so well researched and rehearsed. They can believe in me and what I say. The next year I speak about Wiremu Tāmihana, the Māori rangatira. Again, I win, and at the school prize-giving receive a silver cup.

But I'm not quite as good at leaping over the vaulting horse made of wood and leather and with a wooden springboard when the whole assembly hall is cleared of the pupils' benches for the gym equipment. We must wear horrible bloomer shorts called rompers, which have elastic round the legs and make you look like a pumpkin. Why can't we wear shorts?

Lining up outside to go into the assembly hall one day, a girl talks about the Beatles and their haircuts. Who are they? John, George, Paul and Ringo Starr, the drummer. They have just brought out their second album, *Meet the Beatles!* So, we all must twist and shout, whatever that is. From the photos, I think I like Paul the best. Though I still hanker a bit after Pat Boone.

One day at the Sunday lunch table, Dad says, *Janny's getting quite pretty.* I burst into tears and rush out into the hallway and into my bedroom. I know I'm not. I'm fat and ugly. Mum tells me later Dad is quite upset. He doesn't know what to say to me anymore. It's always wrong.

Another day I wake up before I wake up. I am flying around way up high, everywhere, so incredibly happy, with other creatures all flying around too — we can go anywhere we like. Then I feel a kind of pull or a tug as if I am joined to something below me. It is my body lying in the bed, still asleep. I think, *If I don't fly back in and put her on, she'll be dead.*

So, I slip in through the back of her neck, putting on her body as if it were a garment-in-one, putting myself into her arms and legs, with me ending up in her head. Gradually I remember her name, *Janet Mary Kemp*, and what she is like, her personality, what she thinks about, the sound of her voice, who her brothers and parents are and what they are like. Then I wake up. I have put on my earthly raiment. I get up.

The bathroom is next door to my room. Joan teaches me how to clean my face with Pond's Cleansing Cream and a cleaning swab of cotton wool, then we smear Vitamin E cream on our faces to keep our skin healthy.

Because I've always been a bit plump, and don't have a flat stomach like my cousin Judy Pem had at fourteen, I go on a strict diet and try not to eat between meals, or have any cake or sugar, and eat only one helping of everything. I can't tighten my belt as tight as I remember Jill D and her friend Jane P did at Intermediate School to make the boys look at them but, as Mum says, I'm in proportion. It's just puppy fat that will melt away.

Still, Mum is a bit worried, because when she was my age she was also plump and went on a crash diet, so much so that she became anorexic and Nanny had to put her to bed and feed her on porridge. Mum also has one scarred leg, so that although she has shapely legs she puts the good one in front of the other when she poses for photographs. She was walking in the hills with her favourite dog, staying at her cousin's on Pōnui Island, way out in the Hauraki Gulf, when the dog went rabid and attacked her, ravaging her leg. When we were little and lived in Morrinsville and asked,

Why have you got a funny leg, Mum? she would say, *Because I slipped on the icy back steps one winter and dropped the crate of milk bottles and the glass cut into my leg.* She said this so we wouldn't be afraid of dogs.

Judy and I start going to dancing classes in the Howick Community Centre — the girls are from Pakuranga College and the boys come up from St Kentigern College, further away over a hill or two. Our dance teacher wears high heels and a straight skirt and blouse and is very deft at turning and spinning and holding one of the boys as her partner to demonstrate, then one of the girls to show the boys what they should do. We all love learning to waltz and to foxtrot, and the teacher even does the tango, but just to show us how it's done. Dad practises all the steps with me at home in the living room. He's a lovely smooth dancer, holding me firmly, and steering me with elbows held high, so I learn how to follow. As a joke, he can even quickly cross his hands onto each knee and back, just like Gene Kelly.

The end-of-year dance evening takes place in the church hall next to All Saints where Buppa's organ is. I wear a shirt-waister and dance with Brian Harris, who is friendly and nice. I don't love him at all, but he is fun to dance with. I even dance with Greg Steele, who is a year older and sits next to me in the rear car seat when we are driven home. As I get out, I have to duck so as not to hit my head and he says, *Nice back!* But I'm not quite sure whether this is a compliment or a joke — perhaps I don't have a nice front? I'm wearing a coral-coloured organza ball dress to the knee, with a V cut front and back, in which I feel very special.

When the other pupils in 4 Academic A go to Latin, I quite happily go to Art with Nelson Thompson who is a real artist and our teacher. But what a pity there was no Third Form Latin teacher at Morrinsville College, I think, when years later I learn to sing in Latin. It's a beautiful language. So many words come from it. I love saying it on my tongue. How I scoffed at it then, when Judy would practise saying *hic haec hoc huius huius* . . . and I'd say *honc.*

If I'd learned Latin in Morrinsville at thirteen, I'd also have known about the cases and declensions which so foxed me when I started to learn German in the Upper Sixth. At least we all started French together in the Fourth Form and Miss Kennedy let us draw pictures of Chartres Cathedral, and at least there are only two genders *le* and *la.* I can still sing 'La Marseillaise' off by heart.

We have English with Mr McConnachie and read aloud Oscar Wilde's play *The Importance of Being Earnest*, and so meet Lady Bracknell who says *in a handbag!* in a stentorious voice that Mr McConnachie successfully mimics, and we all laugh. But I don't like the sound of the *g* in the name *Algernon* or its shortened form *Algie*, as it sounds like a gurgle going down the plughole in the hand basin.

Young Miss Britton teaches us Biology. She walks past

the classroom windows and her breasts bob up and down — she wears nice cotton straight-waisted dresses — and all the boys giggle. But we listen to her very seriously. As I do to old Mr La Roche, who teaches us Chemistry and how to put a Leclanché cell together. In the end-of-year exams, I come top in Science! This is unbelievable, beating the more scientifically minded boys. I think it's because of my memory — I can see the periodic table of the elements on the wall above Mr La Roche's silver head, all varnished and with a wooden frame — and I just remember them.

Or do I have a bit of Dad in me? He would have gone to Canterbury College and become an engineer if the Depression hadn't happened. Instead, he had to go out and fix sash windows for sixpence to earn a living. And then the war came and off he sailed with the New Zealand soldiers to Egypt. He'd wanted to become a pilot but was tested as colour-blind. This also means 50 per cent of any sons I might have will be colour-blind, because I carry the recessive gene. I learn about this in the Fifth Form when we have Biology with Mr Ralph who wears long shorts to just above his knees and long socks up to just under them in summer, so that when he stands near your desk to correct something or ask you a question you can see the blond hairs on his legs.

We study Crick and Watson, and all feel so excited that we're at the frontiers of science — drawing diagrams of both RNA and DNA and their double helixes. It's just fascinating. I even become a lab assistant along with

Sannij Reijners, whose parents came from Holland. She is incredibly beautiful and has long straight blonde hair. I hate having to, but someone must chloroform the mice so that we can dissect them on wax trays. As Sannij doesn't like doing it either, I do it for her.

But the best teacher of all from the Fifth Form onwards is Griffy. He talks a lot and sometimes tells us stories the whole lesson, so that we don't have to do anything except listen and laugh. He wears a black handlebar moustache and nice light suits and a tie, sometimes even a bow tie. He is light of foot and sort of dances round the classroom making sure everyone is happy. I just adore him.

But then, lining up one day to enter the classroom, I see Ian S lining up opposite to go into the other classroom. Tall and slim and quiet, with a pointy nose, he is just gorgeous. I swoon into the arms of my girlfriends Sue and Rhonda, nearly fainting. I have inscribed his name in spiky calligraphy with pencil on the back of my writing pad and filled it in. I say his name over and over: *Ian S. Ian S.* Once, at a teenage party he does talk to me, but also to the twins in our class.

At least I spend much of the party talking with the very clever Jim Brook who is tall and dark, loves Griffy too, and is in Ian's class — they are a year older than me. Once, Ian gives me a ride home in his little green car with headlamps and drops me off at the top of Mellons Bay Road so I don't have to take the bus. I'm in heaven. But it isn't to be. Much later he marries one of the twins.

Our Music teacher was born in England and has that sort of accent and the wonderful Christian name (though we don't call him by it) of Halstead. It's all very complicated — music. Even though I've passed Grade 3 piano in the Royal Schools of Music exams, you need the mind of a mathematician to do advanced music theory. Though I do try. Also, singing seems to be very much to do with holding your voice well in your body and letting it come out. You yourself are the instrument, with nothing else to rely on, like a pencil and a piece of paper when writing.

Mr Halstead Marryatt decides the school should present a Gilbert and Sullivan opera at the year's end. He's chosen *Iolanthe.* Cousin Judy is to be the Fairy Queen and I'm Phyllis the shepherdess, playing opposite Stephen who is to be Strephon, the shepherd.

We have to sing a love duet together, *Good morrow good lover / good lover good morrow,* up until the triumphant last line, *for we're to be married today, today / yes, we're to be married today.* I must wear a white wig full of ringlets, and a waisted dress with a low-cut bodice and a stiff petticoat under the skirt to make it stand out, and special shepherdess white stockings and black slippers with ties.

My dark eyebrows look a bit strange under the stark whiteness of my wig. But I'm not nearly as dramatic to look at as Judy in her long starry, silvery robe, who carries an enormous wand and comes in from the wings towards her band of fairies and in her deeper contralto voice sings

Death thy doom and thou shalt die! and all the fairies wail and wail as she plunges her wand down like a giant sword.

Because we're going to sit School Certificate at the end of the year, we must have five subjects. Mine are English, French, Biology, Geography and Maths. It's not much use my taking Chemistry and Physics like some of the boys, as I want to do an Arts degree later. I love Geography as much as I love Biology. Mr Akehurst is always early in his classroom, drawing on the blackboard the multi-coloured chalk soil profiles we are presently studying right down to the rock underneath — so that we know what a desert in contrast to a temperate climate's soil structure is like. There are enormous pull-down classroom maps, and at a glance we can see the whole world flattened into two dimensions.

And thank goodness Aunty Mary still coaches me in Fifth Form Maths so that I can keep up with algebra, geometry, trigonometry and arithmetic quite well. In fact, when the School Certificate results come out, my highest mark is in Maths, 83 per cent — which isn't high for a Maths mark — Ralph Marrett gets 99 per cent — but it's easier to get high marks in subjects where it's just right or wrong. In English I score 80 per cent. I've chosen the title 'Fishing' from their list, and my first word is *Strike!* and on I write about the fish catching the baited hook in its mouth. I've known about fishing since I was a child.

I end up with 318 points in School Certificate, the

highest any girl has ever had at Pakuranga College. Anyone who scores over 300 points they are pleased with. And even Mr Ralph, our Biology teacher, who also takes Sports, thinks I should be in the school team for putting the shot. But I'm hugely embarrassed that I've thrown it so far. It's like a cannon ball. I don't want to become New Zealand's Tamara Press. She's the giant Soviet woman who wins at the Olympics all the time.

4.

Up the other side from the Pakuranga College dip in the road and towards Auckland, the Pony Club is on the left. Here Judy rides Gypsy, the pony Gordon Spence our polo player once gave her older sister Elizabeth Pemberton. Elizabeth was first known to us as Ann and being the eldest of the ten cousins marries first. Her husband John is an artist with a sharp nose and a skinny tie and Beatles haircut. Judy and John's sister are the bridesmaids in thick pale-greenish linen dresses. I wear an apricot one with cream edging at the waist and short-sleeved cuffs and one of Mum's cream boxer hats. We all troop into, then out, of All Saints Church in Howick, built in 1847 of wood with scissor trusses and diagonal bracing. Aunty Mary plays

Buppa's organ for them at the service. We are all so happy — it is our first wedding in the family. Who will be next?

Some of my classmates are already talking about the brand of refrigerator and washing machines they're going to have when they're married. I can't believe it. Don't they first want to know what life is like? To explore it. To discover? To think? Some of them have steady boyfriends already who they will one day marry. But they are only sixteen, like me.

I walk down to the end of Seymour Road into the spare section with its patch of bush and trees high on the cliff overlooking the sea. I make myself a nest among the climbing ivy-like plant, and dream and dream, looking at the light fluffy clouds floating way over. From here you can hear the *swish swish* of the waves onto Mellons Bay Beach and the rocks below — the more secluded part that you get to if you walk along to the right from the bottom, off Mellons Bay Road where the ice-cream store is.

An old, rather grubby and very surly couple sells ice creams and newspapers. I think of Katherine Mansfield's *The Woman at the Store* — which we've read with Griffy. The store and its keeper have the same murky atmosphere. I know only that story and *The Doll's House*. I love Else's line, *I seen the little lamp.* I see it too, through her eyes.

The poet we're now reading with Griffy is Dylan Thomas. Do all poets have bulging eyes? *The force that through the green fuse drives the flower / Drives my green age . . . / And I am dumb to tell the crooked rose / My youth is bent by the same wintry fever.* I love the way Richard Burton says *fever* and how his voice goes up on the *-er*, emphasising it. Griffy plays us both Thomas's and Burton's recordings on his own LP records on the school radiogram. Strange that sometimes an actor reads better than a poet. But I like hearing the actual poet's voice. It's a kind of signature.

We also listen, enchanted, to *A Child's Christmas in Wales* and imagine the villagers and the scenes, so different from our New Zealand Christmases by the sea, full of light and swimming and going outside. Though we decorate a Christmas tree still, it's a smaller one now we're older.

There are fewer of us now that we're in the Upper Sixth. Some people left after the Fifth and Lower Sixth Forms to work or to go to a technical school to learn a trade. Those of us in the Upper Sixth have all been accredited the University Entrance examination and are staying on to sit the University Scholarship examinations to give ourselves bursaries. Judy stays on with me, as do Ralph Marrett and dear Henry Toung, whose parents were Chinese immigrants to New Zealand and who also loves having Griffy as a teacher. Susanne Haydon becomes head girl and Ralph head boy when we are all made prefects and can go and spend time in the prefects' room.

I'm more successful at writing poems than being a bossy prefect. Since the Fifth Form, Griffy has sometimes called me into his office to go over the lines of the poem I've submitted for the school magazine *Pegasus*, named after Pegasus, the winged horse in the monogrammed insignia on our green school blazers. Griffy makes suggestions about this word or that.

Already he's taught us so many poems, like James Elroy Flecker's *How splendid in the morning / grows the lily: with what / grace he throws / his supplication to the rose: / do roses nod the head, / Yasmin? / But when the silver dove / descends I find the little / flowers of friends* . . . and on the poem goes about how Yasmin is the loveliest of all. I'm so pleased as we had jasmine growing wildfire all over one fence in Morrinsville, so I remember well its tiny white-on-pink flowers and can see them in my mind's eye when Griffy reads us the poem in his sweetest tone of voice.

But my own poem that wins the Poetry Prize is much more brutal really — about a death. But then I remember the last line of Flecker's poem, *For one night / or the other night, / Will come the Gardener in / white, and gathered flowers / are dead, Yasmin.*

Thrush

Our cat got a bird
only a thrush-bird brown & swelled in its bird-fluff belly
only a thrush with its orange-curl beak

and its orange-stare fearful eye.
I found feathers, spilled grey fluff & dead leaf feathers
spread as a wind holds leaves —
all torn feathers, dress of a bird
which steamed pulse-fear, hot fear
through skin to skin of my own wet hand.
His side-eyes gaped in an endless stare,
though my round nest-hand was warm.
I found him late, for his wing was gone
& his moult was plucked by a cat of the jungle,
a bird-cat catcher.
I found him late & the half bird died.

But I say to Griffy, *I can't change a word, can I? The poem just came like that, arrived as it did.* Thinking, if I change a word it might all fall apart like the pile of sticks that I remember from playing Joss Sticks up at the Whitianga bach. Griffy very carefully explains, *You can, if you find a better word or a less lumpy (if you want less lumpy) rhythm here or there.* He's so helpful. It feels so special, being a poet.

Because I'm to receive quite a few prizes and silver cups at the end of the year, the Geography Cup, the Biology and Poetry and English prizes (all books), Miss Kennedy calls me into her Senior Assistant Mistress's office to explain she'd like me to look very neat and tidy. To please make sure my blouse is tucked in and my skirt isn't skew-whiff, and that I'm wearing my blazer with the Pegasus monogram proudly. I hadn't realised I was such a messy girl till then. Afterwards she almost apologises by saying to me, beaming with pride, *You did that beautifully.* Even though from behind you can see I walk like a duck, as my father does and maybe because of Mrs Murdoch's ballet lessons in Morrinsville.

Miss Gray is the newly arrived, first-ever teacher of German at Pakuranga. It's a special extra subject we're allowed to take for the Scholarship exam. It's probably because of the sound of the word *heimweh* that I first love German — you can feel the longing in it. I also love words like *plötzlich* with its plosive beginning and soft back-of-the-throat *-ch* ending, not to forget the fascination of having to put an umlaut on some vowels and say them differently.

We study from a little red book called *Aufenthalt in Deutschland. Aufenthalt!* Such a long word that only means *stay*. It's a *portmanteau* word — there are so many in German, they remind me of an engine with all its carriages being pulled along by the main word, which in this case is *halt* or *stop*. The trouble is, though, Miss Gray likes standing up in front of the class — there are only seven or eight of us — and giggling. She hands out magazines called *Schöner Wohnen* for us to leaf through.

But I'm not interested in how to decorate my living

room or which curtains and cushions to buy. And I'm just hopeless at German grammar. It's very hard to understand the cases when in English we only have the genitive left, as in *the girl's boater*. Judy is much better at it, as she's had Latin since the Third Form and tries to explain it to me.

It is to be my downfall. At Scholarship I score only 18 per cent in German, which isn't even added into the total. You must score at least 20 per cent. So, instead of getting an A Bursary, as Judy does, I get only a B Bursary. That's £50 per term less. Which is a lot. I will still need to work in the holidays again, as I've been doing since entering the Lower Sixth. I've been picking strawberries early in the morning before school on the farm out towards Whitford.

Sometimes I'm so tired I lie down between the rows and hide behind my punnets in their wire basket for a quick nap. Or I serve ice creams at the top dairy in Howick, just below Stockade Hill and opposite where Mum works again in an accountant's office, doing his books for him. Joan also goes visiting older ladies in their homes or rest homes around Howick in the little pale-blue Morris 1100 Dad has bought her, taking flowers or a book or just to talk to them for a little while. I often think we are so lucky to have such a lovely mother.

An American boy, a Field scholar, invites me on a date. It is my first date! I am now sixteen. Mum and I carefully plan what dress I shall wear — my straight

Morice, Janet and Joan (on the steps), 7 Seymour Road, Howick, 1966. PETER KEMP

purple linen one with the pearly, pointed, quite high-heeled shoes. Arden is supposed to come to collect me in the small sports car he is so proud of. (I wish it was Ian S in his little old-fashioned green Ford!) Unfortunately, Arden's sports car has broken down and I can't let my pink chiffon scarf stream behind me in the hood-down car in the wind — but then you're not supposed to do that either or, like Isadora Duncan's, it might wind itself round the car wheels and you'd be strangled in an instant.

Instead, we must go and come back in the brown Howick bus. We're to go out to dinner in the Italian restaurant at the top of Symonds Street where Arden has booked us a table. I've never been out to dinner or to a restaurant before. The head waiter welcomes us and ticks off Arden's name in the book at the reception and smoothly leads us through the restaurant to our table. The carpet stops just before it, and the floor beyond is wooden — perhaps it's the dance floor, for there's a slightly raised stage big enough for a band just beyond the tables. I've tried to walk in and sit down elegantly, but with a whoosh I sweep all my cutlery onto the wooden floor with such a clatter as I sit down that the other guests look up at us. How inept. They all can see it's my first time ever.

Luckily, Arden is that kind of American who can cope with such things. He comes from Iowa, where nothing ruffles you — not even the wind on the prairies, as he says. All is calm and blond and made of hay. Perhaps I ought to marry him and go back to Iowa and have a Whirlpool or

General Electric refrigerator and washing machine instead of Kelvinators? But I don't love Arden. I do, though, truly love Ben. Benny. Ben D. Benny D. He has left school now and is an apprentice draftsman in an architect's firm. He didn't go to our school, but to St Kentigern College down the road, where Sam Pillsbury, the other much more film-star type of American than Arden, also goes. Benny is dark-haired and dark-eyed and dreamy and somehow bashful and sweet. He has eyes like the Kennedy family, eyes that if they look up you can see a tiny glimpse of white underneath. This isn't a good omen. It means sadness. And Benny can be sad too, I know. I can just feel it.

One evening we each wander down to Mellons Bay Beach — he from his Bleakhouse Road ridge, me from our Mellons Bay Road ridge — meeting intuitively in the middle. We go along a bit where it is less open and sit together on the shells and sand, leaning back against the cliff. We talk and talk about the stars and what their names might be. We are very philosophical. And we kiss. Because we are in love.

Benny wants to do it, try it out, as he knows Sue and Rob have done, as I know they have, because Sue has long conversations on the telephone with me about it all. How they kiss you. Whether or not they put their tongue in your mouth or yours in theirs. Where they are allowed (or not) to touch you. But Mum has said to me, *Save it for marriage, darling.* So, I say now to Benny, *I can't. I'm not allowed to. I can just kiss.* And so, we just kiss and hug, it seems endlessly. It is wonderful. But I can see he is still disappointed.

It gets quite late. We walk back along the beach and back onto the road. He is going to walk me home. Then we see the headlights and I recognise Mum's Morris 1100 coming towards us, with Dad driving and Mum in the passenger seat. *Get into the car, Janet*, Dad says. So, I do, waving out the back window to Benny as they drive me back up the slope to our house.

But it's not the end. He's allowed to come visit me at home, in the living room, rather than on the beach. He puts one of Mum's Beethoven Symphony LPs on the radiogram and we lie down on the floor, our heads on our arms. He's turned off the living-room lights. He says, *Now be quiet, just listen.* But after about ten blissful minutes Mum comes in saying, *You two must keep the light on, please.*

In the front entrance hallway, there is a little tapestried-back wooden chair and the telephone table. I often sit there having long whispered conversations with Sue about what boys do. Sue knows everything and I'm just learning about it all.

We swan around the school playground together during the morning or lunch breaks arm in arm like a team of two, meeting and greeting. Sue is best at it. She seems to know the whole school and always smiles. I'm learning fast about the social whirl. But one day I see Berris McMinn, still in a classroom, in her circle of plaits and ribbons. She is reading *Little Dorrit*. I read the title as we peer in through the window, giving her a wave, then we flash on by. In my heart, I know how brave and clever she is. Her family are Quakers. They live at the top of Pakuranga Hill on the other side from the Howick side.

Griffy rightly thinks very highly of Berris and she is near the top of the class. But her parents won't let her join the carload of girls when Griffy collects us all to go to a special five o'clock session at the Lido Cinema in Manukau Road. We see some of his favourite films like *Wild Strawberries* and learn a lot about the director Ingmar Bergman. We see death in the face of the tall blond actor Max von Sydow in *The Seventh Seal* and watch *The Silence* with bated breath.

But the moment of moments comes when Griffy takes us to the Russian *Hamlet*. And there he is in person, outside the Lido Cinema where they also show Film Society films, the Russian Hamlet himself, Innokenty Smoktunovsky, with straw-like blond hair and wearing a Hamlet shirt in a sort of cream calico that falls off the shoulders and without a collar and with a tie string. With a large group of other onlookers, we all gather around him outside the theatre, and he signs some autographs and we all swoon and love him from the first moment, not to mention the film.

Sannij brings a record to school. It's the music Mikis Theodorakis wrote for the film *Zorba the Greek*, which Griffy has recently taken a group of us to see. We just love dancing like Anthony Quinn and Alan Bates, all strung out in a line around the classroom, the desks and chairs pushed back, our arms held up and clicking our fingers like castanets. We feel as free as they do and just as tantalised by life itself. We too want to live, enjoy and feel free. Griffy follows up on our adoration for Anthony Quinn, and we all go to *La Strada*, feeling heart-broken and touched, watching Fellini's wife Giulietta Masina playing her role as Gelsomina. What would a life on the road be like for one of us? Is it possible here in New Zealand?

Griffy tells us we ought to not immediately get married and have washing machines and refrigerators and children, but to travel — to canoe down the rivers in France, to live on a kibbutz in Israel, to make love in the lupins on the New Zealand beaches, being careful not to get pregnant but to do it in the open air under an open blue sky.

We are now learning how to appreciate a poem. First, you read it aloud to hear the music of it. Then you read it again carefully to yourself, silently. Then you ask yourself three questions in this order: *What is the poet doing? How does he or she do it? Is the poem successful?* You are not supposed to say *I like it* or *I don't like it* straight away, for that means you haven't even given the poet a chance to be heard. It's a useless and meaningless response. You must justify your reading with evidence from the poem to support what you think.

We start to read some of the Metaphysicals like George

Herbert, Andrew Marvell and John Donne, whom we especially love when Griffy tells us the joke about *John Donne, Anne Done, un-done.*

But I think my favourite poet of all is William Blake. *Piping down the valleys wild / Piping songs of pleasant glee* . . . I don't know why I love *Songs of Innocence and Experience* so much, except that they just sing to me, as do Blake's illustrations. To me Blake is a true wild poet hearing the sounds in his head, seeing the images in his mind, writing them down and painting them. And the fact that Griffy tells us he and Mrs Blake would sit in their garden outside their thatched cottage and take their clothes off in the sun.

5.

Mum and Aunty Mary's only and younger brother, David Hooton, comes home to New Zealand with his wife Margaret, a former biologist, and their daughters, Frith and Brighid. They have lived all over the world because Uncle David, a physicist, has had jobs at the university in Edinburgh and in Göttingen at the Max Planck Institute. Both girls speak with English schoolgirl accents, every word pronounced perfectly.

David is to be the Professor of Theoretical Physics at the University of Auckland, and they buy a house just over the harbour bridge at the bottom of the hill that leads up to Northcote. It has a garden that goes down to a stream, and you can see up the whole gully and hear tūī and other birds and see them flying up through the flax and rushes when you stand on the veranda.

Aunty Margaret makes almost everything herself — out of felt, cotton, silk or other natural materials. She weaves and spins and cooks vegetarian foods and, like Joan, reads spiritual books such as *The Cloud of Unknowing.*

When Mum and Dad enrol at Aunty Margaret and Uncle David's recommendation for the first year once-a-week evening course at the School of Philosophy Inc., which hires upstairs rooms in a building at the corner of Eden Crescent in Auckland, just down the hill from the university, I go too. It's not Dad's sort of thing really — he'd rather play billiards *up at the club with the boys*, though he does go along for the first term, as he likes meeting people and being charming to them.

We register, are put into a group, and sit and listen each week to a lecture read by someone from behind a desk. Then we make our *observations* on what has happened to us during the past week when we've tried to apply some of the school's teachings. Much of it is about learning to *pay attention*, with little maxims like *Let your mind fall on the moving surfaces* when we're working with our hands, to help us learn to develop detachment from the task. Also, to learn not to identify with the voice in our head that says *I*. Because there is a much bigger *I* behind this that is the seat of consciousness.

It is all too much for Morice, who decides not to continue after the first term but is happy to let Mum and me go. I am then given a second evening a week, when I must serve tea to one of the groups. And do so, paying great attention to the cup, the pot, the pouring, the handing it to the person, the gentle asking if they'd like to have milk or sugar. Afterwards we wash up the cups and dry them by hand and very gently put them away.

It's all come from the London School of Economics and the efforts in the 1920s of people like Orage, who studied Ouspensky, a Russian, and Gurdjieff, an Armenian Greek, and through whose teachings two of their disciples, Mr MacLaren and Dr Roles, made contact via the Maharishi Mahesh Yogi with the Shankaracharya of the North, who gave them the nod — a link to a kind of apostolic succession of spiritual knowledge — so that they could found their two schools, the School of Philosophy for Mr MacLaren and the School of Meditation for Dr Roles. The movement spread like wildfire all around the world and came to Auckland from Wellington where the first New Zealand School of Philosophy was set up.

And we are all taught to meditate. And, at a special ceremony, when Mr MacLaren comes on a visit from London and we all go to a teacher's home, one by one we are each given the *mantra*, a magic word whispered only into our own listening ears, a word we must never repeat except silently to ourselves when we are meditating. I learn only later that George, Paul, John and maybe Ringo meditate too.

Then there is to be a long weekend camp at Ōtaki, which Mr MacLaren will lead. We travel down by car and stay in the many bunk-bed and other rooms of a hostel for three days and nights. Again, we are put into teams for the day. One team is told to wash all the long and many curtains in the big hall, then dry, iron and re-hang them. They are so relieved when the job is done. Then the instruction comes: *Do it all again.* So, they do, paying attention to any grumpy feelings that may arise within them, and letting them pass, letting their minds fall on the moving surfaces and developing detachment.

At night we peel all our own carrots and potatoes and vegetables and cook the meals together in the large kitchens in our teams and after we've served the others and we've all eaten together in the long dining hall, we do all the dishes and put them tidily away.

At one evening lecture there aren't enough chairs for everyone, even in the big hall, so I sit on the edge of a table at the back, near a strange bespectacled man called Russell Geary, who is a brilliantly gifted pianist, everyone says, letting our legs dangle down. I'm fascinated by Russell Geary, and I've never met a brilliantly gifted pianist before.

Mr MacLaren asks for our observations after his lecture by saying, *And how does that feel?* And I say, *I feel as if I'm swinging in the void with my head chopped off*, which isn't a very helpful observation, and I suppose they're all thinking I've made it because I'm sitting on a table next to Russell Geary. Afterwards, I'm given an audience with one of the tutors, who ascertains I'm perfectly all right and should really have sat on a chair where I'd have been much more comfortable.

In February 1968, aged seventeen, and with just a month to go before my eighteenth birthday on 12 March, I enrol as a student at the University of Auckland, taking English I, Philosophy I and, because Judy and everyone else is taking French I, I take German just to be different.

During the first term, I travel in and out from home on the big brown Howick bus. But I want to go flatting, and at the start of the second term I find a room in the old wooden mansion at 60 Grafton Road with its footbridge from the pavement to the middle floor. And it is Mr MacLaren who tells my parents, *Let her do it, she'll be looked after.*

1967

—

1969

1.

Number 60 Grafton Road was on a slope on one side of Grafton Gully that slices down the hill from Auckland Hospital and Grafton Bridge all the way to Auckland Harbour — with the Domain fanning out and up from the Stanley Street tennis courts on one side and up to the Museum, and with the University of Auckland spread along the other ridge. It was a walk down to the crossing and up Grafton Road past the two narrow Victorian wooden buildings that housed Auckland University Press, where the publisher, tiny, bespectacled, and famous for once having been a blue baby, Dennis McEldowney held command.

Then, on up to the crossroads of Grafton Road and Albert Street with its great plane trees and through the gardens and courtyard behind the Clock Tower Building that faces Princes Street and Albert Park and on into the upper or lower lecture theatres for English lectures.

Or, diagonally opposite the Press, into the grey stucco German Department on the pavement side of Grafton Road and at the Wynyard Road corner, where the tall, dark-haired and dashing Prof. John Asher, who I always muddled up with Goethe, held court. There you had tutorials in smaller rooms and groups, a favourite being Jochen Neuberger's language laboratory, because he was so blond and so German-looking and so young and handsome. The only way to cope was to look at his rather short feet, ensconced in slip-on shoes worn without socks.

Herr Neuberger's voice would suddenly boom into your earphones as you sat in your cubicle trying as hard as you could to pronounce the difficult umlaut accented words, pursing your lips to say *Über allen Gipfeln ist ruh*, trying to say the *ü* in *über* quite differently from the *u* in *ruh*. It was a matter of getting the unaccustomed vowels and consonants into your mouth and getting your tongue around them. *Über* . . . *ü* . . . *ü* then . . . *u* . . . *u*. And of pronouncing *-feln* as just one syllable and not saying *-felen*.

Having switched to your booth, Herr N would suddenly intone into only your earphones. He was now speaking to you alone, not everyone at once, and so, startled yet pleased, you would try to repeat what he'd said, and think of his short shoes so you weren't overwhelmed by his handsome face at the control console you could peep at through the glass front partition of your cubicle.

I loved reciting Goethe's poem in my head over and over as I read it, until I knew it off by heart. When I saw Caspar

David Friedrich's *Der Wanderer über dem Nebelmeer* I knew I'd found the exact aural image for the back view of that blond, tousle-haired, no doubt wide-faced man in a flaring, dark-green velvet frock coat and boots with his walking stick stuck into the high rocks, staring down and over the clouds and mountains below into infinity.

It was a new joy, just as was Anna Marsich showing us Brueghel's *Fall of Icarus* painting as we read W. H. Auden's 'Musée des Beaux Arts' in our English I tutorial, held in a room just around the corner from the stern, grey German Department. We discussed the poem line by line. Miss Marsich asked us individually and politely to comment, *And have you something to say, Miss Kemp?* And gradually we overcame shyness and tried to express our yet unformed thoughts into an observation.

It was uplifting to leave the tutorial and walk back along Wynyard Street to the cafeteria for lunch where, if we were lucky, we were served by Jack S's wife, the beautiful Anne, who with Jack already had a little daughter. Knowing how poor we mostly were, she'd wave us past the cashier box, ringing up £0.00 on the bell, having served us a plateful of not very tasty mashed potatoes, vegetables and a slice of corned beef or a boiled egg, and we'd collect that and a set of cutlery wrapped in a paper napkin from the wooden box and go to sit and eat it at one of the big tables in the dining room.

In Jack's circle, to which I belonged only as an occasional, peripheral visitor, was our Kiwi spitting image of John Lennon, 'intellectual' John B, who so often was there on one of the laid-out mattresses in the huge wooden-floored living room of the house at the end of Akiraho Street, which Jack S had simply occupied as a squatter. Out would come the drugs — usually marijuana, sometimes hashish — and Jack and John and any bearded or long-haired friends would gather and while away an afternoon, smoking and sometimes, especially John, imparting the great wisdoms of life to lesser beings, the hangers-on.

On an empty wall in their squat someone had scrawled *Madness is infinite perception.* It troubled me. Did I have to go mad to be able to perceive the real truths about life? Are there any to perceive? Must I take drugs to raise my consciousness even though the Philosophy School had strictly advised against it?

Anne and Jack lived in a spacious flat near the top of Parnell Rise, behind and across the top of the street from Parnell Library, with a view downhill over the colonial wooden houses to the harbour and the wharves with their containers and container ships and the sea. I supposed he paid for the rent for his little family by dealing drugs, as he never seemed to have a job, as Anne did with her cafeteria one. I once even lay down beside him on their bed, listening to his philosophising, marvelling at his insouciance and soft brown curls, thinking, I oughtn't be there in Anne's place. *She doesn't mind*, he'd protest mildly, smilingly. *I've trained her not to mind.* Which made her sound like the disciple I was being turned into.

I had other outlets. A very tall man would bend down under the beam in the basement coffee bar where I worked part time, serving coffee and apple tart to students who had come for a gossip after their lectures. Tony Curry was much older than we all were, had an English accent and light-blue eyes and a long space above his lips to his nose where the two folds come down — he would purse his mouth in a certain quizzical way and answer with great earnestness as well as glee.

He was studying Philosophy, wanting at last to graduate with an MA, and also read Chaucer, just for fun, loving it so much he had taught himself Middle English. I learned this after I had visited him two or three times for a return coffee at his tiny flat just down Grafton Road on the corner opposite the German Department but along from the English Department when he started to quote to me *Heere bigynneth the Nonnes Preestes Tale of the Cok and Hen, Chauntecleer and Pertelote.* I can recite the lines to this day, up to *in al the land, of crowyng nas his peer.*

Above him in the same building lived the formidable other English literature tutor, Riemke Ensing, partner of the musician Bill Trussell. I had been careful to put my name down on the list for Anna Marsich's class, not Riemke's, as she seemed to me so fearsome, but the minute she put up a list for anyone to join her in a play to be rehearsed and staged in the theatre, I couldn't resist.

I loved Brecht. Judy Pem had by now moved into a flat upstairs at No. 60 and brought with her a Kurt Weill record of *The Threepenny Opera*, and anyway we had begun reading *The Caucasian Chalk Circle* in our German drama course. Judy and I would prance around her flat, singing and acting out Mackie Messer and Pirate Jenny, her record player spinning out the fantastic jazzy notes and words full of threat and darkness, light, shadow and a great German word, *schadenfreude*, a word we both loved pronouncing.

But it was not *schadenfreude* I felt on the stage when the curtain finally went up on the first presentation of our play: it was stage fright. I could not remember my opening line. So, I sat there, petrified, on the park bench in the middle of the stage next to two other young women students to my right, all of us dressed as old ladies, and wondered what on earth to do except stare, unmoving, at the audience. Luckily for me, it was the actual stage instruction. Don't move. Stare. Then the student sitting in the middle got up, walked deliberately to the front of the stage, turned and walked even more deliberately out and into the wings. I was perhaps next? But what were my lines?

The other student spoke to me. She must have been Vi and I was Ru. *I see little change*, I replied. Thank goodness I have a good rote memory and Miss Ensing had rehearsed us well. Then I followed suit and left the stage, as the third student then did, the stage empty except for the park bench. Then we all came back, but Vi and I had changed places. Flo was still in the middle. It was Beckett's *Come and*

Go. A *dramaticule*. Not wordy Brecht at all. And my lifelong friendship with Riemke had begun.

She was born a European, a bone of contention with her, because of Hitler and the Third Reich and how her family had had to escape from Holland. Though I'm unsure of the exact details — that's her story to tell. And hers was only one of many Dutch families who immigrated to New Zealand in the war years or soon after. It was of huge appeal to me to know someone who had come from somewhere else. What was their story? What was Europe like? How could you ever go there and walk on land where for generations thousands of feet *have trod*? How would you even earn the money to pay to get there — it was such a long way away.

In my first year at university, I joined the Students International Club. I was fascinated by the Malays in their colourful costumes and headgear, the Indians, even if perhaps only from Fiji, not the real India, in their saris. I was moved by the general feeling of goodwill with which they related to one another and to me.

Patrick was a handsome, older Indian law student, always immaculately dressed in a jacket and tie, who lived downstairs at 60 Grafton Road before I moved there. In my first term I sometimes used to visit him for chats in his room. You entered under the walk bridge off the lower pathway through the heavy main wooden door with its stained-glass inset window which let some light into the lobby. His room was on the left; a set of stairs on the right led up to a leprechaun-like physicist; and at the back, in what later became Michael Morrissey's family's rooms, resided the cigar-smoking philosophising Jim du Bignon — the same age as and friend of our older cousin Ann and her husband, the painter John Buckley.

The room that eventually became mine was up that narrow staircase. But you came in through the front door over the walkway, again through a wooden door with leadlight stained glass in it, often too heavy and slightly off its hinges to be able to be properly shut. The wide lobby led to the painter Robin White's room on the left, and mine to the back right, then another flight of stairs and up to Judy's attic, which she moved into once the other painter, Claudia Pond, had got married to Peter Eyley and moved out, going to live in their big, sprawling house in Mount Eden with a workshop off the garden in which Peter ran his garage and everyone got their cars fixed. Claudia, born American, was a year or two older than us, and was so friendly, so open and casual in a way we tongue-tied New Zealanders weren't. She showed us her white wedding coat with a hood that she had embroidered with coloured flowers by hand.

Once you entered my large square single room with one sash window, you'd see my bed against the wall in the right-hand corner and walk past my desk on the left and on the right Dad's small gramophone lying on some bricks with my pile of LP records propped up against it, and then take a step down into the small hanging-on-kitchen whose whole back-facing wall was covered in small windows braced by thin white-painted and peeling struts. Beyond that was the three-storeyed fire-escape, just holding on by its hinges. You hoped you'd never have to slide one of the two huge windows open wide enough to climb out of, for they were old and very stiff, and you left them open just a crack to let the steam out from the gas-burner stove and to let in some fresh air.

Nobody tended the back garden which led down to a stream and tall eucalypt trees until Julie Burns dug a small vegetable garden behind her bottom-floor flat directly underneath mine. There she lived with her boyfriend Ivan, who could have been Russian or French, and who once fell asleep in the bath, in the only bathroom — and toilet — in the whole house. There was an old gas califont which you had to heat up to get the hot water to fill the bath through the long copper piping and shaped pourer. At the time Ivan fell asleep, he had been reading Hospers' *Introduction to Philosophical Analysis*. On waking up as the water got colder, he realised he'd dropped the book, fished it from the bathwater, and wrote on the flyleaf *Hospers floats*.

And next to Ivan and Julie on the lowest floor were Keir Volkerling, even then an ardent environmentalist, and his wife Ngahuia, who after their divorce changed her name back to Te Awekotuku and became an activist for lesbian and Māori causes as well as a renowned academic. She had a slight lisp and sometimes wrote and performed her poems at readings.

2.

The peace movement was in full swing, and Picasso's 1949 peace *Dove* was so well known the world over that Robin White painted an even simpler outline twenty years after that. I wrote a poem celebrating the idea, having been transfixed by the painting hanging on her wall.

The white dove

Only the white dove can grow
from the flower eye,
the seed of the symbol,
& from the lush curve of the calyx
be born — the dove is the lily
the dove is the white jasmine
the dove is the pure flower.

The eye is buried
beyond our way of seeing,
the way of the blind
& from our inward eye alone, we may
be born — the dove is the lily
the dove is the white jasmine
the dove is the pure flower.

The flame will blind your eyes
but the flower will open them.

Some of the thought in my 'white dove' poem must surely have come from the weekly Monday lectures for my group at the School of Philosophy, which I still attended. I also still attended on Thursdays as a tea lady, serving the tea, collecting up the cups and saucers and cake plates and washing them in the sink, drying and putting them away, trying to let my mind *fall on the moving surfaces*, and not babble and chatter away in my head or talk to the other helper so that silence should reign while the lectures in the three rooms were being read out.

There was Uncle David, with his rolling gait and pleasantly deep, softly echoing voice, a senior tutor; there was Aunty Margaret, observant as a blue jay, not that we have any in New Zealand, ready with a spicy comment before you could say Maharishi Mahesh Yogi. There was Mum, smiling and being nice to people.

Certainly, the Philosophy School's advice — *Do it on your own through attention and meditation — don't take drugs; they will only set you back at a level lower than your consciousness was before you took them* — was very good advice, for me at least. I wasn't sure if some of the people I knew took drugs or not, and I was still a novice when it came to alcohol.

Lyndsay B with his elegant black chin beard and

moustache, exotic as his Italian surname, and with long, manicured fingernails on his right hand, was my classical guitar teacher. How I paid him I can't think — perhaps I read or calligraphed him a poem? I wasn't that good at guitar playing, though I'd managed to buy myself a guitar that was stored in a beautiful black case. I had the red and green guitar books — for beginners and intermediate — and just adored playing.

Once Lyndsay brought with him a half-filled bottle of wine — *Liebfraumilch* — and to his great surprise out of the kitchen I produced my own half-filled bottle with the same brand name. To celebrate after the lesson, we gradually drank the lot, perhaps with some chunks of cheese and toothpicks and crackers I'd found in my safe, for there was no fridge. That night I puked my guts out into the kitchen sink, feeling so rotten, sick and sore in the stomach, I vowed never to drink *Liebfraumilch* again, despite the pretty nun in white and blue on the label and it being a word I could translate from German. And so it has been.

Besides its political articles, *Craccum*, the university student newspaper, sometimes published a poem or a short story. So, still in my first year at university, I took a typed-up copy of my first ever story, 'The Wooden Blocks', to the *Craccum* office which was upstairs above the University Bookshop, and tentatively handed it in.

I had written it imagining the chunks of wood

delivered before each winter to the end of our driveway in Morrinsville from a wood supplier's truck and dumped in a heap in front of the garage. I used to help Dad stack the pieces away along the sides of the garage and at the back, carefully fitting them so that they would not tumble off. Some had thick bark, and some were cut into oblongs, and some Dad would split into kindling to start the fire. It was a job you felt your way along with, so I suppose that's why I made Erith the protagonist blind. Though why she should burn the blocks at the end of the story — blocks so lovingly made for her by her father and hand-polished by them both with sandpaper to make them smooth — I don't know.

The editor accepted the story. I was now an author. A short story writer. Published, and perhaps read? It felt wonderful. And I knew I needed another mentor, as Griffy had been for me at school, but where would I find one?

In English I, our lectures included 'An Introduction to Shakespeare' by Mac Jackson, held at 10 a.m. on Tuesdays in the huge lower lecture theatre, where from up the back looking down over the tiered benches and through the long clear cathedral-like windows you could see the occasional lecturer's wife delivering him and his leather briefcase when he was late for his lecture, then popping the children who'd tumbled out to help back into the car to drop them off at school on her way home.

Everyone loved Mac because he was gentle, he knew

his Shakespeare, and he laughed or rather chuckled as he lectured. I decided he was it. I should try to be assigned to his tutorial class in English II. But no luck. I was assigned to C. K. Stead, who I could see was terribly clever, but I felt with his clear, stainless-steel mind he would cut right through any observations *Miss Kemp* might tentatively make and she'd be in slivers. Boldly, though inwardly trembling, I asked the departmental secretary if I might instead attend a Jackson tutorial and was granted that favour.

To reach Mac's office you walked over the little stone bridge near the back of the Clock Tower Building. This led into the stairwell from the lower to the upper lecture theatre, so you went in and up the stairs, then, instead of turning right into the theatre, you went straight ahead and around the curve of the building, with the offices all on the left, facing Old Government House.

Come in! Mac would boom from behind his desk, with the emphasis on the *in*, his back to the window and facing the opening door, at your tentative knock. And in you'd go, new poem clutched in your hand, though later I'd often leave them in advance, in an envelope slipped under the door, so he'd have time to read them before I came to ask him what he thought, and we'd discuss it.

Once he left a note for me on the door in an envelope stuck with sellotape labelled *Miss Jan Kemp* in his amazing-looking, almost backwards as if medieval handwriting. Inside there was a little note. It read *I liked this one very much. You seem to get everything right, just by instinct.*

Mac. I was over the moon. It was much better than the remark on my William Blake essay, when I'd written *Mr Blake* and Mac had circled *Mr* and written in the margin *This word is otiose*. I'd had to look up *otiose* in the dictionary to find out what it meant.

Mac taught us all how to fold a *duodecimo*, which Shakespeare's printers would have used, numbering the pages so that once folded, paginated, printed and stitched they came out in the right order, though when you spread out the single large piece of *duodecimo* paper the paginations seemed to be all over the place, totally at random. Mac was also a sleuth with concordances and proved who had written which parts of *Arden of Faversham* by analysing the vocabulary and the typefaces, for some single type-pieces would be broken and recognisable when they were reused by the writer's printer. This statistical work contrasted with his wonderfully heart-felt reading of Shakespeare's sonnets.

Karl Stead inaugurated a Friday evening drinkies session in the bar at the top of the building near Constitution Hill, where Sam Pillsbury, who had lived next door to Benny D in Howick, flatted with some friends in a house built halfway up the very steep hill. I popped in there sometimes and once saw Benny D again, and we had a nice chat. He was working in an office in town. Not the kind of person Karl would know or invite to the drinkies. No, it was his mate, the historian Keith Sinclair, and people like Michael Morrissey, with his rumpled curls and friendly, intoning, never-stopping ramble of thought, and who was now our rent collector at 60 Grafton Road and so earned himself free lodgings for himself and his wife Dot and their daughter by being the janitor.

At one of these meetings Karl said to me *And when are we going to have an affair, Jan?* I knew he was just being clever, so I managed to be just as clever and answered him, *When you take the same emotional risk I would, I will, Karl*, which shut him up. I hope he was impressed by my quickness of wit. I was. I learned lots from Karl, though — once I told him I couldn't possibly attain, sustain and retain the amount of knowledge I really should. Very wisely he said, *The things you need to know will come to you and stay with you. The rest, you just let fall away.* Those words have come back to me so often — just do your own thing. The rest will take care of itself.

So many puzzles to consider and conquer and accept, learning languages and whole new subjects I'd not encountered at college. I'd opted for Art History I as one of my first-year courses, and went into the big, darkened lecture hall once a week to listen to Herr Flaschtig in his bow tie showing us slide after slide after slide — about fifty per lecture — in his introductory course *From Greek Art to the Present Day*. It's an absolute eye-opener seeing all these hundreds of slides, week after week, but I know nothing about art.

I can remember the names of some of the artists and the titles of their paintings no trouble, and slowly start to identify them — Leonardo's *Lady with an Ermine*, a black-and-white print of which is propped up in a plastic folder on my bookshelf, or Cézanne's black lines for a tree, *Une arbre.* I can remember my French from the days at school quite well, so that helps when the paintings' titles are in French.

By the time we get to the end-of-year exam I just scrape through with a C+ pass by writing an essay about the connection between medieval mosaics and the broken surface of one of Picasso's portraits. Herr Flaschtig writes in his report on my work *She knows nothing about art, but her leap of the imagination in connecting these things is highly original.* Hooray for me. No one wants to fail. But I know I'd better not continue with Art History. I'm not good enough at it. And when you consider, what a lot to digest in your first year of study.

Gradually I got to know many of the people who lived up and down Grafton Road from No. 60. You'd see them leaving home or returning, just as I did, going down then up the hill to the university and back. And even some who lived up by Auckland Hospital past the crossroads at the top, leading on to Grafton Bridge which spans the gully.

Michael Neill and his wife and daughter lived in Grafton Road in the house just down from Dennis McEldowney and Auckland University Press. Judy Pem was in his English II tutorial and loved his wit and presence. Later Michael moved to Brentwood Avenue, in Mount Eden, next to the little park. Sebastian Black and Judy Binney taught at Auckland too, he a lecturer in the English Department and she in the History Department. Judy was also the daughter of the wonderful Head of English, Sydney Musgrove, who I always got muddled up about, thinking he was King Lear. Michael, Sebastian and Judy then lived as great friends and next-door neighbours in Brentwood Avenue just along from the Hell's Angels motorbike gang behind their corrugated-iron fence.

Two gardeners, Mike and Bob, later moved in and rented Michael's old Grafton Road house. We students loved them. Mike, with a dark beard and hair, looked as if he were straight out of *Lady Chatterley's Lover,* which we were all reading. He would stand with one hand on his shovel, his head tilted slightly back so that his beard jutted forwards, as does Monsieur Courbet's in the painting I so loved on first seeing it on the screen in one of Herr Flaschtig's lectures — *Bonjour, Monsieur Courbet.* Monsieur Courbet is out for the morning, carrying his easel and paints on his back, and meets his patron with his servant and dog. The beginning of realism.

With his more golden look, Mike's mate Bob was a kind of gardening fallen angel. Though rougher. Manly. Strong. With muscles you saw rippling as you passed him tending the rose bed and turning the soil.

A seemingly mad American girl, Karen, a little older

than me and with a battered black bicycle, seemed to be Bob's or was she Mike's girlfriend? She was so often there — or seen flying down the steep part of Grafton Road on her bike. I liked her immediately and put her into my poem 'City Sequence': *the black-haired bicycle lady wore / a waterproof canopy / took off like a balloon: / they spoon-fed you, indiscriminate flashes.*

Once, though, Mike took a bad turn while having a trip. Was it Bob or Karen who alerted some of us at No. 60? We came trooping down the road and kept vigil all night at Mike's side — alternately he was warm, cold, sweating, needed a shower, was frightened or shouting at whatever hallucinations came to him. It wasn't much fun at all, but we got him through it and left after Bob had made us all a breakfast coffee and Mike was sleeping peacefully.

Opposite the dairy halfway up Grafton Road and a few yards up from No. 60 on the left-hand side stood 81 Grafton Road, another nineteenth-century wooden edifice, also three floors high with fire-escapes and balconies, its many rooms inhabited by Auckland University students. Judy Pem and I made friends with Callam R, four years older than us, a brilliant microbiology student. Once she and I decided to visit Callam in his room, and we three lay on the bed, Callam in the middle, turning to kiss each one of us in turn and gently fondle us. I didn't look at Judy and she didn't look at me, but just let him. And, we loved it, being stroked *down there.*

At the time of the Apollo II moon landing in June 1969,

Mike Fudakowski, who later married Robin White, lived at 12 Grafton Road with his flatmate, the clever Peter Walker, who later moved to London, wrote for the *Independent* and became a novelist. Some of us crowded up the stairs and into their tiny living room where together we watched black-and-white TV as Neil Armstrong took, as he said, *One small step for man; one giant leap for mankind.* We were out of our trees with excitement. Astounding! Peter got out the binoculars and peering through the open window we all laughingly tried to see Neil on the day moon, knowing it was impossible.

3.

With Dr Kathryn Smits in German II, we are now reading Thomas Mann's *Tonio Kröger*, a slender volume that makes me think we might just manage to read it all before the end of term, for it is slow going, page by page, line by line. Each student has a turn, first reading a few sentences aloud in their best German accent, then translating them verbatim into English.

My copy is marked in pencil where I've looked the words up and written in the English translation, but it's the word order that's so funny, the verb in German coming in second position or, if it's in a subordinate clause, at the end of the sentence. My mind feels each time as if it's going into reverse and then plopping things to fit into the right slot, whereas when speaking English I don't have to think, just speak.

Not to mention trying to note the *der*, *die* or *das* and realise you use the twelve ways to say *the* depending on whether the noun is nominative, accusative, genitive or dative, and singular or plural. And beyond that, after which preposition which case is used. Damnation! Thank goodness for John A. Asher's *The Framework of German* — a little grey handbook, only sixty pages long and with its succinct explanations and tables to learn by heart. *Der die das, den die das, des der des, den der den, die die der den.*

I find it easy to learn words by heart. But to apply them? Then you must think. And that little train shuffles along in my head from right to left, the engine pulling along carriages containing declensions, verbs in all their forms, the whole shebang from which I choose this or that to nut out and put in a sentence to put my mouth and tongue around and come out saying, as if I were Caroline W.

Why is it that Caroline (who also has another W with another surname, both separated by a hyphen, which astonishes me saying it — a double-banger and *two* W's) can speak German as if she were *Thomas* or *Tonio*? The words just tumble out of her mouth as she translates, streets ahead of us all in pronunciation and understanding and translation. How come? In the oral class we learn she has visited Germany in the holidays, sailed up the glorious Rhine and has even seen the Lorelei, which we know is a huge rockface with girls singing on top, and she also knows about the Rhinemaidens in Wagner. How did she get the money to travel? We are just students, all poor or on bursaries topped up by holiday jobs as posties or working in a factory.

I've just spent the summer in the chocolate-topping factory in Newmarket, daily flicking labels out of the machine and wrapping them onto the plastic bottles of chocolate topping that come by on the conveyor belt. One of the older women must be in her sixties. She's been there for yonks and is the head of the union and is asking for a rise in pay. There is a real hierarchy among the workers — who is on top, who has been there longest, who works fastest — and they show a certain jealousy of us, the young students who can escape and go back to be further educated and get better jobs eventually, and not be stuck in a chocolate-topping factory all our lives.

A fellow chocolate-topping worker who is studying at Elam art school has made a dark, wooden sculpture of a little band of people, joined in a row as if they've emerged from a coal-mining disaster. He gives it to me, and I give him a copy of my poem about the white dove, handwritten, for I like calligraphy. It is for him to frame and hang on his wall. I treasure the little sculpture and put it on my windowsill.

The job I enjoyed much more I found in the following

summer holidays, working at Robin Lush's printing press, near the Kiwi Tavern on Wakefield Street. I would stand at the folding machine and with one finger regularly push forward a new slice of paper and, like a drummer, at the same time step down on a lever with one foot. The paper was then taken in and *kerchong kerchong* neatly folded twice — a leaflet for the delivery boy to distribute in the city centre. If you got your timing wrong, the machine would choke and jam, causing an awful mess of ripped paper, which Robin would smilingly unjam until I learned the trick of it all. I watched him patiently hand-set the type in the big press, choosing the single letters and carefully setting them into the right slot.

My room at 60 Grafton Road costs £4 per week. Michael Morrissey comes round on Saturday mornings to collect the rent and tick it off in his little blue notebook. I only have about £10 a week to live on, which isn't much, remembering too that Judy has more, as she got an A Bursary and has a Studentship because she's contracted to become a secondary-school teacher, something I couldn't bear to sign up for, not wanting to be bound. My silly B Bursary status haunts me. They should have counted my 18 per cent in German in Scholarship, as we know, but they didn't.

The youngish couple in the dairy sell all the usual to the students — including the proverbial meat pie, often a dinner staple as it doesn't cost much and fills you up with its meat and pastry. But it's not healthy. Sometimes I try to cook a few carrots and beans on my old gas stove with its four burners. Or fry a chop or a piece of fish or make an omelette. But on £6 a week, unless you're very inventive and walk all the way down to the markets and back, there isn't much to be had.

And here am I, stupid me, still persevering with German. But I love it, the *Klang* and the percussive sound and Goethe's poem *Es schlug mein Herz, geschwind zu Pferde!* The immediacy and energy there on the page for you to see and to hear when you say it aloud. Could you say that in English? Could I? I'd have to turn it all around.

And anyway, what about *Es wurde getanzt*? Not from Goethe, but just said. So *passiv*! How can dancing possibly be a passive activity? Not that we danced, or did any exercise, except for walking up Grafton Road and back lugging our satchels.

My cousin John (remember Tamber John Richard Pemberton and the little red leather wooden-handled strap?) is a year or two ahead and in the Maths Department, very cleverly becoming a tutor. He and his girlfriend have joined the tramping club. They are so wholesome, far too wholesome for us intellectuals. They have knapsacks on their backs and stout boots and socks and go wandering in the Waitākeres, probably singing *I love to go a-wandering*. No, we aren't goody-goodies, as we think John is. We want to know about life in the raw. About sex and love. About protest and ideas of the mind. Though John does tell me, probably much more importantly now I think about it, that *computers will change the world.* And does his best to explain to me what one is.

I have a boyfriend, David T, a few years younger than me, who sometimes comes and lies with me in my bed. One of his lovely brown eyes wanders a bit when you look at it — blinking back at you. I think he reminded me of Benny D from my teens. We aren't much good at making love. We just lie there and talk mostly. David is best friends with the university tutor and poet Kendrick Smithyman's second son, Stephen. They had both attended Westlake Boys' High School on the North Shore, together with Christopher D'Arcy, I later heard, my very first childhood love from Morrinsville. Christopher was on the stage as Azdac in *The Caucasian Chalk Circle,* the Brecht play Judy Pem and I so loved when we read it in German class — *Der kaukasische Kreidekreis,* with the wonderful wild judge who sat on the law book on the stage, on top of what seemed a tree-stump and dispensed justice.

Kendrick Smithyman himself is a sort of Quasimodo figure in the English Department, with his rumbling, grumbling voice, always talking to himself or anyone in earshot. Once, visiting him at his and his poet wife Mary's home, as she read us her famous poem 'Wife to Husband', he let me stroke the cat he was holding lovingly in his arms and seemed, too, to purr himself.

Michele Dales, with her curly gingery hair, has come up from Wellington to study at Auckland and she becomes my German II class companion. We address each other with *Guten Morgen, gnädige Fräulein* and write notes to each other signed *deine Freundin* — and sign off thus on email to this day. She has become an exceptionally fine watercolourist, using black ink drawings as a basis for her pictures, and she is a weaver of note.

Michele is huge fun and lodges in Wood Street, Freemans Bay, in Rod and Eva's house, paying for a room with a high bed up a ladder under the ceiling to help them with the rent. Eva, a secretary at the university, is of delicate build with a pale face. Rod, much heavier and with a dark beard, calls her *my Princess* in a way Michele finds both cloying and possessive. And when Rod, an Anthropology student doing his Master's thesis on pipi middens, shoots at the blowflies attracted to the festering heaps of pipi shells in the back garden with his air rifle, Michele thinks he is a bit cracked. He calls everyone around *Fucking hippies*. Perhaps both things are the reasons Michele gets herself a pair of Dracula teeth to put in and scare him with. We take mad photos of each other in the garden, wearing them among the flax and avoiding the pipi middens.

Michele has a Buddha-like, independent, balanced nature and is such a kind, dear friend. She is always unusually dressed in colourful costumes she has made herself, and round her waist has a homemade leather belt in which she keeps her tobacco to roll into a durry if she wants to have a smoke. And it isn't always tobacco. But luckily Michele doesn't know Jack S and Anne or John B. So, it wasn't mescaline or cocaine but just the occasional puff of marijuana, as far as I know. I love her love of the bizarre and the comical, the exotic and the ordinary. She even makes the fishmonger feel at home when she buys fish from his open-air truck on Ponsonby Road.

4.

My older brother Peter, like John our cousin, was also studying Maths and somehow managed to save up his Studentship money to buy himself a beautiful apple-green Citroën Traction Avant, with its huge headlights and dashboards and low-slung shape. One Sunday during my first year at Grafton Road, he parked outside, came in and said, *Come on, Jan, let's go home to Howick for lunch. Mum and Dad are expecting us.* I was astounded. *You mean, we can go home?* I asked. Almost brimming with tears. After all, I'd left.

As a child I sometimes used to think I must have been dumped on their doorstep in a shoebox and they'd taken me in. Perhaps it was because I was dark-haired, whereas the boys were fairer in colouring. But then, I reasoned, I was more like Dad, till his hair went silver, and they were more like Mum, though I know she put a rinse in hers to give it a bit more colour than just mouse-brown, as she called it.

Dad had saved up for each of us in the Building Society fund he paid into for years and years so that when we went to university to study, he could transfer the dividends into our own bank accounts to supplement whatever Studentship or Bursary we might have earned for ourselves. And after that, he wanted us to manage on our own. He was an older father, born in 1905 and, having gone to war, a late father — forty-two when Pete was born, in his forty-fourth year when I was born and forty-eight when Ian was born.

When he and Joan moved to 131 Bleakhouse Road, Howick, from 7 Seymour Road, it was into a smaller house, with just one tiny spare guest room, plus the front porch off their large bedroom which Joanie used as a sewing room or Dad for an afternoon nap on the narrow bed. He didn't want our things cluttering up the place any longer and must have disposed of his war trunks and all that was in them during the house move. Downsizing. Dad wanted the place just for Mum and him — their little nest to grow old in, where he could mow the small front and back lawns, potter over the cars in the carport, bringing each out into the front driveway to wash and polish till it shone to his satisfaction, family off his hands and out of his pocket.

He would even start telling stories about the war when they sat together in the living room at about six every evening — he serving them each a sherry from his decanter and she him peanuts in one of his wooden bowls. Joanie would put on a cheerful face and try to change the subject. She'd heard all the stories before. And she knew it hadn't all been quite as jolly as he was remembering it.

It was a lovely lunch, just as if we'd never left home, Pete had never been to boarding school and, if Ian had been there too, we would have been just us, the Kemp family as we'd been for so many years, having a special Sunday roast lamb lunch in Morrinsville. I knew, though, Dad being older now, that he was glad to have retired and to just live there simply with Mum, her roses growing in the front garden bed and his sweet peas growing along the fence at the back of the sloping section where you could look down and way over towards Howick Beach. Dad had a little workshop at one side of the back terrace that led off the kitchen. All his trusted nails and screws were there in little upside-down green-paint-topped jars. All he had to do was unscrew a jar from its lid and take out the nail or the screw he needed. Such an orderly man.

At last, I get one of the most coveted holiday jobs — as a postie. And in summer I walk all the way down to the Chief Post Office, Auckland, for my training sessions and eventually part of the way back up Anzac Avenue then down onto Beach Road, delivering to all the businesses and car-repair shops as I go, then round under the railway bridge past the bottom of Parnell Rise along the Strand to near the bottom of St Georges Bay Road, my heavy canvas bag gradually becoming lighter. Once day near the end of my run a huge transporter truck driver comes careering towards me as a joke, as if trying to run me over. He veers away at the last second but gives me a real fright.

Within a few weeks I know all the postbox and letterbox numbers of every firm by heart, so I am quick at sorting the mail. And then I'm outside in the fresh air, sometimes in the rain, and can think my own thoughts as I trudge along. On another run a black dog jumps out at me from down a driveway in Parnell, so I swing my postie bag round and round to ward it off, until the owner hears my shouts and calls it home and takes it by its collar. I realise I had been thinking about Joanie's leg on Pōnui Island, hoping mine wouldn't be mauled too. Despite this adventure, I still like dogs, though apart from Peppy have never since had one as a pet.

5.

I am nineteen. I've written a little poem called just 'Poem' for my new boyfriend Hank who has a small room in a Wood Street house. Hank isn't one of the *fucking students*

Rod complained of who inhabited so many of the houses up and down Wood Street. Not to forget Herman G, the ginger-haired old man who ranted and raved at the pub and wrote poems too and was counted no doubt by Rod as one of them.

Hank is a motorbike mechanic and a sailor, a friend of Judy Pem's boyfriend Archie. They both work at the motorbike shop on Ponsonby Road. Hank wants to save up and buy a yacht and sail to the islands of the Pacific Ocean. Somehow, I fall for him — he is gentle and quiet — and I visit him. We lie in his room and make love. The poem is about afterwards.

Poem

A puriri moth's wing lies light in my hand —
My breath can lift it —
Light as this torn wing, we lie on love's breath.

As a young woman student without a permanent partner the main thing is not to get pregnant. It is most worrying sometimes waiting for your period to arrive — sometimes even two weeks, the time probably having been extended by the worry. So, some of us have gone to Student Health and asked to be put on the Pill. This has done away with those horrible rubbery condoms, and you feel safe. (It is still years before AIDS surfaces.) The only problem is the side-effect of putting on weight — one of the horrors of my life, having been a chubby child with that tendency.

And we weren't yet in 1973 with the introduction of the mini-Pill which, so long as you never forgot to take it every night, solved that. Freedom! You could then choose how to live your life. Already a doctor has told me that it will be quite hard for me to conceive anyway, as I have an introverted — upside down — uterus. That too is a relief.

Somehow, the thought of becoming plump again was frightening to me. And if you were pregnant, you'd necessarily swell out, balloon-like, and then be bound, like an umbilical cord is bound, to blood, the flesh, the looking-after, having to take your baby to the crèche while you went to lectures — I knew I couldn't cope with that. Besides, I had my poems to write. And more of them were slowly arriving as babies perhaps do, though in my head rather than my belly.

I wrote a poem intuiting I too was a sort of mystic, whatever that was. Some words I just wrote down, because they came, then I had to look up the meaning to see if it fitted.

Mystics mild: Song

That slow moon hangs full under the faint twig
when cats' cries beat the night air thin to the tender ear.
Under such guise, those whose images long to spring,

must wait for the sea's long suck
to make the kelp rise up & spawn lank tresses,
the giant sea flower opens.

Revere, revere all mystics mild,
the bright-tongued mouth
the sleep-eyed child.

Mother! You tether me too close!
Your cornucopia is to soothe the child of me
in your great lap, slap my back to hear the cry,
I am bound to you forever.
But in my free kingdom, I slip your fetters,
ride fleet sound into the waves.

Revere, revere all mystics mild,
the bright-tongued mouth
the sleep-eyed child.

And it was true — it was the sounds in my head I heard, listened to and sometimes wrote down, escaping from Papatūānuku, who as the concept of the Earth Mother I adored, but to whom I did not want to be tied physically by bringing forth an offspring to offer her. I was hugely grateful later when Cathie Dunsford, a great supporter of my writing, sent me a homemade Christmas card onto which she'd written the titles of all my poems up to that date, and inscribed *Dearest Kempi, Happy Christmas, with love from all your poems.* It was a real eye-opener to me. My poems were my offspring.

And later still, when Aunty Margaret, who in my eyes had become a sort of mystic, soothsayer or seer, and who so often helped me during my life with aperçus of a spiritual nature and life guidance, said *You didn't have to do that*, as if it were an enormous task I'd been relieved of, leaving me free to try to discover myself and just to be a poet.

Of course, then a woman poet. We were still very chauvinistic in the late sixties. Even me. All my language was so. After all, we students went to the Kiwi Tavern at the top of Wellesley Street East on the Symonds Street corner every Friday night to mix and mingle and talk and have a drink — *the six o'clock swill*, until it ended in October 1967. What a relief not to have drunken and sometimes spewing men sprawling out onto the pavements, some landing in the gutter, from where a patient girlfriend would wipe his face and, despite his protests, heave him up again, throw his arm round her shoulder and totter him home.

In English II I made friends with the gentle Martin S. We were supposedly studying Shelley's *Prometheus Unbound*, which I couldn't really understand because of the high-flown language, but Martin seemed to. So, we'd sit in the coffee bar over our books and cups of coffee, and Martin would help me, until his girlfriend Marilyn, as tall and willowy as he was, came to fetch him.

With Mac we were both reading *Hamlet* which we adored, loving its language, loving its sadness and drama, loving poor Ophelia even as she drowned, as Shelley too did; feeling sorry for Shakespeare who had lost his only son Hamnet so young that he had to write a play. And we could see it all — for the annual outdoor Shakespeare production the battlements of Elsinore Castle being well served by the turreted wing of the Clock Tower Building and the stage being built onto the grass lawn with tiered seating for the audience in the courtyard. There, way above against the Milky Way and the moon, Hamlet's father's ghost could roam and say *Remember me!* It was hauntingly good.

It was in the study period at the end of term and before the exams. Judy and I had invited Mac round to see our house and to have afternoon tea with us. I think he was astounded not to find us sitting there quietly, each in her own room, dutifully revising, but upstairs in Judy's, blowing bubbles. She'd bought a bottle of bubble soap and wire loops and said we should have some fun. Mac joined in and we happily blew bubbles, drank tea and ate a home-baked cake Aunty Mary had given Judy.

After the exams, Judy then found a part-time job helping Mavis, who had an antique second-hand shop near the top of Symonds Street. Judy was always a gatherer of things, with a real collector's eye. It was she who had her eye on Buppa's carved wooden rocking chair after he'd died, and his goods were to be divided among the family.

I hadn't thought of it and was a bit shocked, in mourning for our sweet gentle grandfather, that we should think of his chair. But Judy knew worldly things are important too. She moved out of 60 Grafton Road to live in the flat above the shop, to be on hand if Mavis went out during a lunchtime and generally to help, earning a bit of much-needed cash. It was a good arrangement for each of them.

Judy didn't seem to go to the student parties I went to. She had Archie. But I went. And at one such very druggy party suddenly an older man with a dark beard and moustache and a slight accent was turning his blue eyes on me and being kind to me.

I don't know what I'd smoked or drunk, but he put his hands on my shoulders and said, *Reality Jan, reality.* I truly didn't know what reality was. We had to live so much in the imagination if we were to write poems, if we were to read poets and write essays about them. What was reality?

6.

Gradually I learned what this was. Johannes Maria Caris used to draw up outside 60 Grafton Road in his pale-blue station wagon with a long rooftop to carry a ladder on. He'd come to New Zealand as a Dutch immigrant, and first registered as an electrician on 13 May 1959. He was much older than me — twenty-one years and three months older, to be exact. He had been born in Weert, in southern Holland, in 1927 into a Catholic family, the youngest of four children.

Now he lived in a small fibrolite bach on a large bushy section at 42 Tainui Road, Titirangi, in the Waitākere Ranges. If you parked in the carport opposite the low wooden letterbox, you would first go along the bushy part, then over a wooden slatted bridge above a small stream and on down the path to the bach door.

The fact that he was Johannes Maria and I was Janet Mary felt like named destiny to me. But I didn't much like the sound of Dutch — it seemed like flattened German lying on its side, its vowels not as round and full. But his Dutch neighbours, a cabinetmaker, Joop Boortman, and his wife Willie and their three young sons, were so welcoming and such fun to be with. Willie would make potato chips in hot oil in a wire basket on the stove and often invite us both round for dinner. Joop looked a bit like Yogi Bear and was funny, gentle and generous. The boys played happily with us all — card games, board games, simple family stuff. This indeed was reality.

Hanging on the right-hand wall above the bed in Johannes's bach was a concave wooden shield covered with studs, regularly enough placed, though you could still see it was handmade. Johannes told me the story.

His parents had had two red brick houses next to each other in the same street in Weert — in one was his father's wine merchant's shop with its big barrels in the cellar; the family lived in the other, along with an old aunt and a maid. On 12 January 1944, Johannes's eldest brother Loet was caught while evading being manpowered into work under the occupying German Nazi forces. He was already twenty and certainly didn't want to work for them. He said he'd left his papers at home.

Once there, he managed to escape through a back door. Loet had dreamed of becoming a pilot, but the war made that impossible, so instead he focused on electrical engineering, and had built his own radio which he'd hidden in a wine barrel, allowing the family to listen to the forbidden Radio Orange.

During their search of the Caris house for Loet, officers discovered the radio and resistance leaflets, so both his parents, Frans and Maria Dorothea Wilhelmina, as well as his seventeen-year-old brother Huub were arrested, and the men eventually taken to Dachau, where Frans died of typhus three years later. Maria was released a month after her capture but, as her house and everything in it had been confiscated, had to find alternative accommodation for herself, her daughter Toto and Johannes, who had been away at school at the time of the raid. The two brick houses were taken over and the occupying forces moved in. When freedom eventually came, they moved out in such a hurry that they left their studded shield hanging on the wall. Johannes found it there when he returned home, and kept it as a reminder of what his family had been through.

The story moved me deeply and all my sympathy went out to the Caris family and all the other families who'd suffered in such a way. So, this was what my father had fought for. To free the world from such things ever happening again. I told Johannes about Morice and his expeditions with the Sappers in the desert against Rommel in the Egyptian desert, and they talked about it when eventually I took Johannes to meet my parents at 131 Bleakhouse Road. Johannes had bought himself a blue serge Frenchman's cap and had a cigar. He alternated between sips of Morice's sherry and puffs on his cigar, trying to impress everyone by blowing out smoke rings.

My father didn't really take to him. But by the end of my second year at university, Johannes had invited me to live with him in the bush bach and I'd moved in. We'd wake up every morning to a Beethoven LP played on his radiogram. Johannes had a large collection of records and loved classical music, and though an untrained electrician who had faked his own papers on arrival in New Zealand, he'd soon learned as apprentice to another Dutchman how to connect things up. He'd set the recorder arm ready to play the evening before, the timer to seven in the morning, and there we'd be — Beethoven and birdsong all at once, even before breakfast.

And the meals! Wiener Schnitzel in breadcrumbs fried

quickly on each side with a fried egg on top, together with French fries done in his special basket like Willie's held into the oil. All supplemented on our large plates by a fresh salad. No wonder I put on weight.

Right next to the little kitchen in Johannes's Titirangi bach was a walk-in shower, which he loved using. And loved coming out of, rubbing himself dry, then walking around with just a T-shirt on. He asked me to make him a skirt, so I sewed him a couple of miniskirts, one of which he would hook around his hips and wear without underpants. He also hated to wear shoes and went around summer and winter barefoot — his feet large and cracked. But he was happy.

Telling me he was a nudist, he invited me to the nudist camp one Sunday. We had lunch outside some people's caravan — everyone stark naked except for me. I didn't want to see them or him always without clothes. Not that I was prudish, but I felt awful. I thought nakedness was reserved for lovers.

As well as Willie and Joop, Johannes had some good Dutch friends. Arne Loot, the photographer who lived further up into the Waitākeres near the old Dutch Kiwi restaurant, as well as Andrew van der Putten, the potter at Oratia, where I sometimes used to go to try to learn how to throw pots. Because I wrote poems, he suggested I decorate a pot by writing on it, so I inscribed *this is my porridge bowl for starting a new lovely day.* Once I helped him light the kiln and later wrote a poem, remembering the sparks that flew when we lifted out the side brick to see the kiln was burning nicely inside.

Old railway guard

The old guard
sat in the old charred shed
on a brittle wood chair
& he smoked as he said:
how yer couldn't beat
those old steam trains,
yer couldn't lick 'em.

Standing with his shovel
shoved deep in the coal
with the firebox flaming,
one slow sure bend in his back
he kept that fire burning
all the journey he'd feed it.

The yellow hot flames
shot out like sprouts,
out from those uncut
black diamonds:

and when a li'l dust of wind
caught 'em or you stoked it
with the long pole iron,
there'd be sharp yellow sticks
like coloured rain flyin'.

And yer hair 'd be tarry
and stuck down on yer head
with the sweat:
but yer eyes 'n yer teeth
'd be shinin'!

I discovered that diagonally across the road from the Boortmans my favourite professor Mac Jackson lived with his wife Nicki and their young son Cameron and the baby Anna. To get a ride into the university without having to go on the blue Titirangi bus into town then walk up the hill would save a lot of time, so I summoned up the courage to ask if I might phone Mac each morning and ride in the car with him. Very kindly, he said that this would be fine. So, daily I'd phone to find out if and at what time he'd be leaving, walk round the corner into and along Ngaio Road, and wait at the top of his driveway.

Cam was always belted into the back seat and a great talker, entertaining us admirably with his sometimes rather comical thoughts — very articulate and loud, as much as his father was articulate but quietly so. He would drop Cam off at kindy or at his mother's house in Remuera — she would come to the back door, lean on the doorjamb and greet Cam as he raced up the steps, full of a story to tell her.

Once or twice Mac and Nicki would ask me to babysit so they could go to a Film Society screening at the Lido Cinema in Epsom. So, the two children fast asleep, I sat in their living room all evening, reading, or gazing at the black-and-white photographs of stone figures on either side of the fireplace until I curled up on the mat and slept too.

Many years later I wrote a poem and on its first appearance dedicated it to Anna, who herself has become a fine poet.

Babysitting

Two and twenty
there were runes in the room
it was in the woods
the babes made no sound —
my mother said that I never should
play with the gypsies . . .
my mother said:
always keep a little oil
in your lamp.

Curled round a candle
with Celtic men hand in mouth
foot raised graven in stone

in a huge b&w photograph
before me — we flickered on
trance-like, all asleep.
Plato might well have approved.

There were a number of students who used to run around the university in a gang, wearing long blue-black capes and floppy hats, following their loud friendly leader Tim Shadbolt, whose book *Bullshit and Jellybeans* was released in 1971. He would hold forth over a megaphone on Jumping Sundays in Albert Park — and was once arrested for saying *bullshit* in public. Johannes and I sometimes used to join in, sitting on the grass having a picnic and then wandering about listening to the various speakers in the band rotunda and the rock bands spaced all over the park. And there was dancing and drug-taking. Make love not war.

Johannes and his Dutch builder friend Tony designed an addition to the bach — a step down onto a huge concrete platform surrounded by proper footings made up of concrete blocks with steel rods coming up out of them. There was to be a new slanted roof with clerestory windows looking into the bush garden, and a ceiling lined with two heavy dark-oiled wooden beams and quite a few terracotta-coloured rafters at right angles. Tony, fair-headed, wiry and cheerful, came most days and I helped with stamping the freshly poured concrete into the concrete blocks, each time holding the twisted steel rod vertical so that it would stay like that when the concrete dried.

There were to be two huge plate-glass sliding doors and windows at the sides of the lower floor of the split-level living room, then a new downstairs bathroom on the last flat piece of land to the left before it sloped down through bush to the other side of the loop in the road that wound invisibly around Johannes's bushed section. A staircase up and a skylight bedroom would look back over the lower living-room roof and into the top branches of the tall kahikatea that surrounded it.

It was lovely to imagine having so much more space. Every day we used to walk down the steps of the bach onto the concrete slab and look at the growing construction, imagining from the plans how it would be to live in it. Gradually it was built, and we expanded into it.

And gradually the kilos arrived until I was 19 kilos over my 'trim' weight of 64 kilograms. I saw myself in the mirror and could not believe the shape I'd become. It was hugely horrible. I was only nineteen, nearly twenty. Our kind doctor in Titirangi said I now had the body of an overweight, middle-aged lady. The only way out was to reduce — but how?

Then my grandmother Nanny said to Mum and Dad, *Why is she living in the bush with that Dutchman. Shouldn't they be married?* So I suggested to Johannes we could have a great party after the wedding now the big room was nearly finished. And reluctantly he agreed, saying,

I don't really want to get married. Did he fear the legal responsibility? *But*, he said, *I don't want to lose you.*

We set the date for 22 November 1969, the day after my father's sixty-fourth birthday and after the end of my third-year university exams, and booked a time in the Maclaurin Chapel in the university grounds. Johannes Maria was not a practising Roman Catholic any longer and I, Janet Mary, wasn't a church-going Anglican any longer, so the word *chapel* seemed perfect. And it pleased both my parents and grandmother that there was to be an official tying of the knot.

Dad had just one daughter whose wedding he had to provide for, and he did me proud by hiring a large room at Waipuna Lodge, just over the Tāmaki River on the Howick side, near where he still worked for Rob Butcher at Simca & Co. Mum would organise the wedding breakfast. All the family were invited, including Nanny, Aunty Audrey and her friend Brownie who had flown up from Christchurch, the Pembertons, my godparents the Madills, family friends from Morrinsville, my brother Peter with his girlfriend Henriette, Ian our younger brother, my English teachers at school and university, both Griffy and Mac, and some of Johannes's and my special friends.

I went home to Howick and with Mum visited her dressmaker friend. It wasn't to be a white wedding — after all, I'd been living with Johannes for a year — so I chose a woven pink and many-coloured fabric that looked faintly Eastern European. The dressmaker cleverly sewed a long pinafore that I could wear to hide my large shape, and a pretty, long-sleeved pink chiffon blouse to wear underneath it. No veil, no hat.

And then one day, about a week before the wedding, I confessed to myself — it was all wrong. Johannes Caris wasn't the right one for me. Deep down, I knew it. But it was too late to say so. My parents had gone to so much trouble already. It had to take place, and I truly knew it should not.

The wedding day itself was great fun — solemnly we stood before the altar and exchanged rings and said our vows. Then, with Nanny in the middle, we posed for the wedding photos in the gardens behind the chapel. She was thrilled to bits. And, as we farewelled the wedding guests at the door of the chapel as they trooped out, Mac gave me a chaste peck on the cheek and shook my hand, congratulating me. I was over the moon.

The wedding lunch at Waipuna Lodge went according to Dad's meticulous plan, and we all ate and drank and talked to one another, Johannes and I going hand in hand from table to table to thank people individually for the presents given. That evening, the younger people came out to our not-quite-finished new living room attached to the bach, and we all danced and drank wine, having a wonderful party.

Some months later, as he sometimes did, my brother Ian came to stay for the weekend. He was patiently teaching

Wedding day: Ian Kemp, Johannes and Janet Mary Caris, Nanny (Dorothy Hooton), Joan and Morice Kemp, 22 November 1969. PETER KEMP

me to drive Johannes's black VW Beetle. Johannes was quite happy to let Ian teach me, and so was I. It seemed too emotionally charged to have your husband teach you how to drive. Everyone said that. And Ian was a good clear teacher. I loved the little back Veedub. It whizzed up Tainui Road and along the Scenic Drive with me at the wheel, and I passed the licence test with flying colours, even doing a three-point turn perfectly. *You mean turn around and go back the other way?* Zoom, zoom, zoom and I'd done it.

7.

Johannes had cleverly planned underfloor heating of the house, and he had laid all the necessary wires into the concrete slab before it was poured. Some of them still jutted out and into the space in the yet-unclad wall. One night he left his van's battery charger plugged in and sitting on top of the concrete, and we walked around to Willie and Joop's to have dinner and spend the evening with them — playing cards with the boys, chatting, eating. Ian was with us again and it was fun introducing my own brother to the Boortmans, who felt like Johannes's family, having been loyal to him for years.

Johannes had always been fearful of fire and was the

first to raise the alarm — he'd gone out the small front balcony to smoke his cigar, when over the treetops and in the direction of his house he saw smoke starting to billow up and some sparks already flying. Quick as a flash he yelled out to us all to follow him, and when we got to the balcony we could see his retreating figure racing back down the road.

By then we all could hear the Titirangi Volunteer Fire Brigade's sirens and the explosions — the fibrolite of the bach walls had overheated; the whole construction, old and new, must have been on fire. Looking at one another in dismay, Ian and I followed him, running down the road, hoping against hope it wasn't Johannes's bach alight. But you could see it was from the position of the flames and smoke billowing above the bush. Firemen held me back by the wooden letterbox above the path that led down to the front door: *It's too dangerous to go down the path now — please wait.*

So, I waited, seeing Johannes had run down to the very bottom of the road to enter via the driveway and come up to the bach through the bush garden. Firemen were there too and stopped him. When we eventually were allowed to go and look, the sight was devastating. The whole bach and add-on had burned completely to the ground. It was all a pile of grey-black, still-steaming rubble.

As Johannes and I stood there, holding each other and trying not to sob, but sobbing, I felt as if we had been skinned to just our bodies and the clothes we stood up in.

All we owned, all extensions of ourselves, our lives, our personalities, his records, my university books including my green-covered German dictionary, all my Shakespeare texts, my few jewels inherited from Granny Kemp, all our kitchen utensils, the frying pan, Johannes's German shield, the lamps he'd put around the place to have his beloved subdued lighting, the letters from his sister in Holland and the blue Dutch tiles, all my photo albums, my first manuscripts of poems and stories — all, all had been burned, and was now a great charred, smouldering, wet heap on the place where the bach and its extension had stood.

At a neighbour's we phoned my parents, and tremblingly we drove out to Howick, with Ian in the back seat. My mother and father gave us their double bed to sleep in. Ian slept on the living-room couch, Mum and Dad separately in the guest room and the little sunporch. All I could feel glad about was that there had been no baby we'd left sleeping in its cot, no one at all had been burned. It was just things. And they were most probably all destroyed. But Johannes could not believe he had ignited the fire by placing the battery charger near the upper wires of the underfloor heating — they had sparked and the whole blaze had ignited in a jiffy.

Someone in Tainui Road suggested we move into the empty house just two doors up from Johannes's property and brought us spare mattresses and pots and pans and curtains and bits of furniture to sit on and clothes to wear. And as Johannes couldn't bear to look at the devastation that had been his home for so many years, and anyway had to go to work, I used to go and sit on the piles of wood back at the property, and Andrew van der Putten and I would cheerfully throw wood there, fibrolite there, charred stuff there, singing and laughing and sorting it all out, like sailors after a wreckage.

Another of Johannes's friends, Leo Cappel, a Jewish museum technician, tiny, with dark hair and glasses and an intense look, came one weekend and rescued the LP records that he said he could cut on his lathe to the size of 45s, so that at least we could hear perhaps the second and last movements of a symphony on the old turntable someone had given us. It would never match the quality of Johannes's stereo radiogram on which, in his early immigrant days, he had proudly played concert recordings to the Dutch community in a hall in Henderson. His imported Waldorf speakers gave off such beautiful sound.

By then Andrew and I had also sieved through some of the soot and sticky mess and found some pieces of jewellery — my aquamarine birthstone set of two gold hangers, now slightly skew-whiff, on their fine gold chain; my grandmother's sapphire ring set in gold. Leo took everything with him and brought it back cleaned and polished, slightly discoloured by the fire but all still wearable.

A few months later, Johannes rented the brick and tile

house right round the loop in the road that surrounded his property, and we moved in. The insurance on his bach had been paid out, and Tony was rebuilding it, but properly this time — the same design, and the same upper and lower concrete slabs, but with real wood all round, no fibrolite.

Again, we could help Tony with the construction, me jigging the twisted steel rods into the footings. I knew how to do that from last time.

8.

I decided it was time to do something about my weight problem. I discovered Weight Watchers, bought the book, and joined the Weight Watchers' group in Remuera, where I travelled once a week on a Monday evening to be weighed in and given support. There would be a lecture, and all of us there would stand up and say how much each of us had gained or, hopefully, lost since last time. I followed the diet exactly, vowing to myself that after a year I would be back at my 'goal weight'. Weight Watchers said this must be regarded as a lifelong change — once a weight watcher always one — and so it's been for me.

Johannes hadn't seemed to notice or mind my weight too much. Perhaps Dutch women are rounder. But he would hold forth about women, sitting there with his glass of wine in the evening or, as he said, his *kop kopie* at breakfast, complaining about how all the housewives had it so good. They could lounge around at home all day while their husbands went out to earn an income. They could lie by their swimming pools in their bikinis and sunbathe.

Really, Johannes would have preferred not to have to go to work. He wanted rather to be a potter, like Andrew. But he didn't have the talent, so he complained instead. I listened to these endless speeches, not knowing what on earth to do. I was at last starting to think. But I wasn't good at speaking in long sentences.

Then there was the sex — or rather what he would hold forth about sex. How really people shouldn't be monogamous. They should be free to make love to whomever they wanted, whether any of the parties were married or not. Again, it wasn't my wish, but with the free love movement singing in my ears from all the rock songs I had listened to, I felt I had to agree. And anyway, I didn't find him such a gentle lover. And I didn't come very often. Was it my fault? That's when I remembered Hank in Wood Street and wished I could spend the afternoon with him. Though Johannes had also said, *It wouldn't be fair, though, if we practise free love — you're much younger than me; you'll find more lovers than I shall.* I wrote a poem showing my scorn for his idea.

The new people

On her loom she weaves monoliths for ancient tombs.
In his room he reads dust jackets from cover to cover.
Their lovers come on Saturdays at three, stay for tea.
A contended couple in their rented two-car garage flat —
at all costs they avoid arguments, don't want to lose
their fine integral line of modern thought.

My idea of a wasteland of a marriage. But I don't think Johannes ever read it.

An old friend from childhood came to stay for the weekend with her husband. She was tiny and blonde, and somehow I knew she loved sex. Johannes suggested we swap partners and sent the husband and me up into the double bed in the new eyrie among the kahikatea. We could hear them, down below in the other bed, making love, she quite loudly moaning. Upstairs, we clutched each other, sitting up in bed like Hansel and Gretel, lost in the forest, forlorn and forsaken, wondering what on earth would happen next. It wasn't our thing at all.

Nor was it my thing that I would sometimes come across Johannes in the new shower below the eyrie bedroom, naked, showering and masturbating. *Save some of it for me*, I once said. He laughed and kept on, his face showing all the exhilaration he was feeling. I hated it, but what could I do?

Until I came to live with him, he'd only had himself and the occasional client whose electricity he'd come to fix while the husband was at work. Perhaps it was a morning ritual for him, a habit. But it put me off him, his *pulling himself off*, as he called it. And the idea we should have other lovers — it wasn't what I felt we'd promised each other when we married . . . *and to be faithful unto him, as long as ye both shall live*. But perhaps we hadn't said that. Perhaps I just knew the text off by heart.

I decided to ask for advice. Knowing she was something of a psychologist, I poured my heart out to a newish friend, Gail T, who lived with her husband and their two young children on Waima Crescent, past the dairy at the bottom of Ngaio Road.

We had both just started to attend Auckland Teachers' College as trainee teachers. I knew I had to have a job. What could I do with just a BA in English? I had to have training. I'd chosen primary school teaching, as I thought younger children might be close to their own creativity. Perhaps I would teach them how to write poems. Perhaps we could write some together. I'd always got along well with little children, knowing instinctively never to speak down to them or to laugh at them, but to speak with them and laugh with them. Little children love a joke, but they take life earnestly and seriously, and are usually honest. They were the ones I felt I could be with.

1970

—

1971

1.

To reach Epsom and Auckland Teachers' College my favourite route was the back way over Hillsborough, from where you could catch glimpses of the Manukau Harbour before you went down the last long slope, rather than over the more usual New Lynn, Mount Albert suburbs way. If I was travelling with Gail, I'd walk round to Waima Crescent and wait by the station wagon till she and the children came out. After dropping them off at Titirangi School we'd drive the other way via New Lynn, then meet up in the late afternoon to return after a long day of lessons.

Teachers' College was almost like going to school, and I didn't much like that, having been so much more independent at university. Gail was right into the intellectual challenges of the college, because she'd done training as a psychologist and was keen to translate that into the new teacher-training skills she was gathering.

I found it more fun going 'on section', as they called work experience in schools, and listening in as a classroom teacher went through the ropes of a lesson and you observed, sometimes taking over for a twenty-minute stint, sometimes giving a lesson yourself. I was even posted out to Pakuranga Intermediate for a few weeks, just down the road from St Kentigern, where the boys I'd known at dancing class in Howick had gone. I particularly loved a study of Ancient Egypt that I led in my classroom. The pupils seem to delight in learning about all the gods and goddesses and drawing pictures of the two-dimensional pharaohs and other beings, making wall charts with which to festoon the prefab building.

The most tedious part was the constant whistleblowing and bellringing — short sharp electric sounds at the beginning or end of each period, telling us to move on, even though we might all have been deeply engrossed. And the lining up for assembly and rollcalls and listening to whatever was being told to us by the school principal or his deputy head. I hated all of that. If you counted it up, I'd been at school for fifteen years of listening to the whistle blow and the whole catastrophe, as Anthony Quinn as Zorba the Greek so rightly said about marriage. But at least I graduated with a Diploma in Teaching. As Mum had said, *Complete your study. Get those pieces of paper to show to the world, then you can go anywhere.* And Dad, *Finish what you have started.*

Johannes and I were still living in the second rented house, the one below the kahikatea. Somehow, I still sort of loved him. We had a home together. I felt relatively secure. We had music and meals to share. One day his Dutch photographer friend Simon Buis came round for a photo-shooting session. There are photos of me looking moony and love-lost, like a devoted hippie wife, next to Johannes who stands proudly on the concrete slab at the top of the driveway, the kahikatea behind us — Johannes with his long curling dark hair and long black beard and his penetrating blue eyes.

Simon asked me to try out all sorts of costumes, and because I'd lost all that weight, I felt so much prouder of myself than I had been. He even took a portrait of me lying in bed. In another I'm wearing a dark-pink lace dress. Simon said, *This would get you a job in any repertory company.* It wasn't an actress I wanted to be. I felt I was a poet — though after the holidays I would be a trainee teacher.

One day I forgot to take the mini-Pill our doctor had put me on. Amazingly to me, Johannes and I had made love, one very sunny afternoon, outdoors on the now cleaned concrete slab with some rugs under us. I worked all this out later, after I had missed one period, then the next.

But we can't have a child, Johannes said when I told him. *The house has just burned down. You'll have to have an abortion.*

Janet Mary and Johannes Maria Caris, Titirangi, 1970. SIMON BUIS

But that's illegal! I said.

I was torn by the thought of having a real child, by my uncertainty about how long I could stay living with Johannes, about his wish not to have children, not to have to pay for them, take responsibility for them. I decided I couldn't go through with the pregnancy. Our kind doctor took pity on me and inserted a Lippes Loop. He explained what would happen — it would just be like having a period. *It's not murder*, he said *you've only been pregnant for about three weeks, so it's just a few cells, they won't have formed into a foetus yet*. So, I thought, it would be all right.

What on earth prompted Johannes and me to drive down to the Coromandel and spend a day and a night on our friends Bill and Sylvia's yacht so soon afterwards?

We were anchored way out in Kennedy Bay when I started to bleed. They got the dinghy launched and lifted me down into it with a bucket to sit on to catch the blood drips.

Johannes rowed us to shore where his blue van was parked. We drove the few hours over the hilly gravel roads to Thames Hospital, where I was diagnosed and the Lippes Loop removed. I was given a tidy-up and put to bed in a double room, exhausted.

The next day the hospital took a pregnancy test. *We've managed to save it*, the nurse told me triumphantly. *You're still positive. You'll be able to have your baby*. Johannes was adamant. *We don't have a house to live in any longer. We've decided already. No baby now*. And I worried that already the loop might have destroyed some of the baby's cells.

They wanted me to stay there another week to be sure. So, to be able to get away from the hospital and home to our own doctor, we smuggled in some of Johannes's own urine in a little jar, and the next morning I poured it into the bedpan before the nurse came to take it away for the new test. *It's turned negative*, she said. *Well, it does sometimes take a day or two.* So, I was released, and we drove home to Titirangi.

Again, the doctor inserted a Lippes Loop. A few days later I started bleeding again, and it all came out of me — yes, real cells, squelching and oozing along with the blood, much worse than a period. Johannes drove me to a clinic, so I'd have proper medical attention followed by a curette operation to make sure I was all cleaned out.

Have I ever been more ashamed of myself in my life and, at the same time, once it was all over, more relieved? I might have had a son or a daughter. Forever. Well, for my whole life. As I write, my child would now be fifty years old. Maybe that's why now and then I 'adopt' a younger person I get along well with. And, as I thought then, what if the Lippes Loop had grown into the cells which might have formed the baby's eyes; what if he/she had been born defaced by the miscarriage-producing plastic that had now twice been inserted into my womb? Even so, forever I will think, yes, I did once commit murder. In collusion with Johannes. Our own baby. How could I have?

Now I had only Johannes, so much older than me and whose ways of thinking I was more consciously starting deeply to question and find wanting. And I had my education, such as it was, and my poems. That last was something no one could ever take away from me. That could never be aborted. For they came to me without my asking and were my gift to give to the world. I would bear them all, whatever that meant, wherever it took me, always. I would never murder them, nor let anyone else either. I would stand up for them, read them, present them and represent them, whenever they needed me to do so. That was my vow. They were part of me, my raiment.

2.

He had his blue electrician's van to use, so either I'd drive Johannes's black VW the few kilometres from Tainui Road round Scenic Drive to park on the road outside Titirangi School, or I'd walk round just past the dairy on Ngaio Road to the main road and take the blue Titirangi bus a few stops up and round Scenic Drive with its gorgeous views over the bush down to the faraway sea.

My probationary assistant's school room was in the long main building with its sheltering veranda stretching out next to the tarmacked basketball courts-cum-assembly area before the right angles of the bicycle sheds and near the school entrance and the dental clinic. I was completely in charge of Room 4, with twenty-seven Primer 3 children all aged about five and a half or six.

The first and most important lesson I'd learned at Teachers' College was 'control' — the teacher needed to be in control of the class, or the children would run rings around you. And, how to put them into groups, so that you taught to their level one group at a time when it came to important tasks like learning how to read or do arithmetic, whereas they could all work together when it came to art or singing.

So, I established control. It's not easy when you are only twenty-one and have no children of your own and probably little practice at it. Nearly thirty of them! Little boys and girls. One, a pudgy blonde girl, Tamsin P, proved my biggest challenge. She would burst onto another little group, bully her way in and provoke, deliberately wreaking havoc to draw attention to herself. I did my best.

After a few weeks I had a horrendous dream — all the little children and I were in a swimming hole in the bush. Many of the children were bobbing under, and I'd flail across and lift each one up again so as to breathe above water level; then another would start to sink, I'd rescue him or her, and so on — a true nightmare of a dream. I had to make it clear. Somehow, I managed to bawl out Tamsin, give her a real dressing down, make her come and sit right in front of me under my beady teacher's eye when it was story time — and, lo and behold, she obeyed.

She sat there, almost tugging at my skirt or stroking

my trousers to be closer to her heroine. For that is who I'd become for her. Someone who had clearly marked out the borderline of tolerated behaviour. I didn't like to think what happened at home, though I must have met her parents on parents' evening. I was, anyway, home and hosed. No more trouble.

Which meant they could now all learn, especially how to read. I felt it was my duty to teach them that. Having set up groups according to a little test thankfully supplied by the New Zealand Education Department, I put them into groups, each with a group leader. Each group would read or look through and describe, if there were only pictures in it, one of the little books in the *Ready to Read* series.

Then, one by one, I'd call each group to sit on the mat in front of the small moveable blackboard next to my low teacher's chair, and we'd go through the alphabet — *name of the letter A — aye, sound of the letter a- or ah- or ahhh* — with the relevant phoneme then being supplied in a word by one of the children, in answer to my questioning eyebrows. *And, apple, Arthur*, they'd chorus.

I loved them then. I loved their curiosity and pride in discovery. I loved the Education Department's little green teacher's handbook which laid out the lessons from level to level most of all. I only had to teach it, remembering that the word *education* comes from *educare* which means to lead out. So, I tried to lead out what was in them, and they let me. And followed my instruction.

Just as they did when one day during the winter a

Room 4, Titirangi School, 1971. COLLECTION OF JAN KEMP

fog descended. I requested everyone put on their jacket or coat hanging outside on the veranda, and then we set off in single file, stalking our way across the basketball court, down the slope onto the lawn and the playing fields above the bush that edged the school, set as it was in a protected position halfway up against Titirangi hill with its trig station on top, looking way down towards Henderson below it. I'd sworn them all to silence.

We were not to speak. We were to observe, inhale, bite, eat, swallow some fog. We were to listen, hear and remember what it sounded like, if anything. We were to touch it in the air, where it had landed on a railing, on the grass. We were to taste it, then to bring all our discoveries back into the room like a silent snake with its belly full.

One at a time please! Hand up if you want to say something please! They poured it all out, and I wrote all their observations on the blackboard that stretched right across one side of the room. I walked back and forth, so they could all see and hear me from whichever corner of the room. All their words were eventually there.

And now for the images. Still with the children sworn to silence (for a fog is also silent), I rolled out huge sheets of paper onto the little collections of tables, and each group began to draw and design their fog poems and copy down whichever letters and phrases they liked from the blackboard notes. It took us three afternoons to finish the enormously long wall mural, which we then hung all around the classroom, me standing on a borrowed ladder as the different groups handed up their artwork and words.

Then we all read our great 'FOG' poem out in unison. Then one or another child would ask to read their phrase, so we did it again and again, so that we had soloists and chorus. What a great joy it was for all of us. I hope some of them are writing poems still.

On either side of my Primer 3 classroom, I had helpful support. On the left towards the bike sheds was the senior infant mistress, and on the right Margaret Thornley, a kind Lebanese-born woman married to the potter Don Thornley, brother of the fine artist Geoff Thornley, all of whom lived in their houses further up into the bushed roads of the Waitākeres near the Dutch Kiwi restaurant.

In the staffroom I learned the etiquette of following the hierarchy, though the headmaster was a kindly gentleman and the deputy head, if needing to be recognised as such, was a reasonable man. We all joked and laughed a lot at playtimes and lunchtimes, unless we were on duty patrolling the school grounds, carrying our cups of tea that one of the children would then be asked to ferry back to the staffroom kitchen.

At the end of the year, almost a graduate teacher, the father of one of the girls in my class, Lorne, thanked me profusely. *You've taught Lorne how to read*, he said, eyes beaming. *I thought that's what I was supposed to do!* I replied, pleased at the praise. And besides that, I was now earning a small income of my own. I bought not only a pale-blue Baby Austin A30 to drive to school but also, at auction, four colonial Canadian wooden chairs for Johannes and me to have when our new house was built.

But I wasn't pleased with myself in another way, and the chief dental nurse was livid with me, when one of my schoolteacher colleagues — her beloved husband — admitted to her that one afternoon he'd come round to my place after school, and we'd spent it in bed together. *How could you have!* she stormed, to me as much as to him.

I admitted to myself it was an experiment, it was because of Johannes's wish that we practise free love in our marriage, so I thought I'd better try it so I'd know what it felt like if he tried it and how to accept it. A sure recipe for disaster. And I felt terribly sorry for and guilty about the dental nurse. I still do.

The new house was now built, and we moved back into it, taking the four Canadian chairs and a pottery wine flask and mugs that Don and Margaret Thornley had given us — a belated and very welcome wedding present, as all the other pottery pieces we'd bought had exploded in the bach fire.

Later, when Johannes was claiming for insurance on the burned-down bach, I realised that he hadn't increased the premium payments after the wedding with its windfall of presents, nor after the addition of the big new room. This meant we had very little capital to rebuild with. Luckily, because he was married, he could now get an extremely low Building Society loan, and this pleased him. It was all in his name, because he always said it had been his bach and the land his property.

Johannes had a huge copper pot from a former laundry that he asked Tony to erect on a stand at the right-hand corner of the lower open room whose glass doors opened out onto the terrace. From the runnels of the roof above he hung a fat chain, down which rainwater could trickle and eventually fill the pot so that we'd have rainwater for our pot plants. Johannes was particularly proud of a new succulent that took up a lot of space.

Our new front door was split in two, as it were, at its waist, like a barn door, with a bolt to keep the lower part shut and any possums out but air flowing in from outside. You leaned on it and looked out up the path that led to the little Japanese bridge over the nearly non-existent stream up to the letterbox of No. 42, and to the rented carport across the road.

One day I heard knocking and a moaning voice. I looked out over the shut lower door and there was my cousin Ann Elizabeth Pemberton, all dishevelled and grubby. I invited her in, most disturbed, made her take a shower and gave her both a bath towel and clean clothes. *I want to go to the supermarket*, she then said. *I must have . . .* and she reiterated her list of must-haves. I drove her to the Ngaio Road dairy. *No, it must be this jar, not that one*, she said determinedly. *No, this banana, not that one.*

I was firm. *Elizabeth, it doesn't matter which banana and which jar — we're taking these ones.* I paid for them, and we drove home. She stayed a night or two, as I tried to fathom her out and help her psychologically, then, exhausted, I delivered her home to Aunty Mary in Howick. *She needs special medication*, Mary said solemnly. *And hasn't been taking it, obviously.*

As so often happens in a family that has shown brilliance — both David and Mary had been top scholars in their time — someone sometime gets the short straw. Judy and I had so loved Ann's courage and way with horses, and Gordon Spence had admired her too.

3.

One day the phone rang, and it was Murray Edmond, born in Hamilton in the same year as me, whom I knew along with his wife, Mary Paul, of the Paul's Bookshop family, from undergraduate days at Auckland University. Murray knew I wrote poems as well as that story that had come out in *Craccum*. Would I like to come and read some of my poems with other Auckland poets at the new Arts Centre on Grafton Road?

Somewhat trepidatious, I said I would. Some weeks later, armed with a sheaf of poems I'd typed up, I set off for the round concrete building set back from the street almost opposite Auckland University Press and down from 12 and 14 Grafton Road where Tony C, Riemke Ensing and Bill Trussell and others lived.

David Mitchell, a little older than us, with his round ha'penny spectacles and longish black curly hair, was the centre of attention. He had an absolute certainty about his work. He read sometimes in a high voice, sometimes in a low one, sometimes demarking passages in a stilted way as in 'my lai/remuera/ponsonby' to show the contrasts between the dreadful Vietnam War massacre in 1968 and his loved girlfriend *she*, in the kitchen boiling an egg.

Someone, perhaps Murray who was studying Drama and knew how to present things, had suggested we poets should sit on chairs on an upper dais ringed around the circle of the audience, who were divided into segments like quarters of an orange, leaving walkways facing two or three poets in each quarter. We'd *spin a poem*, which meant each poet would read a line from their own chosen poem, then round to the next poet for his or her line, then on to the next, and round and round making a new Dadaesque collision of style, voice, idea and rhythm. The audience lapped it up. We were local stars.

Perhaps Eleanor Horrocks sometimes read, perhaps she didn't. Like me, as a woman reader she was a rarity. All the rest were men. Gentle Bob Orr was there, also a forty-niner like Murray and me. He'd been at school with my brother Pete at St Paul's and his parents had a bach — the Orrs' bach — on the road up the Thames Coast past Whakatete Bay. Bob was now a wharfie and wore shabby dress, so he no longer looked much like a St Paul's boy, but he was a real poet. One from the docks. He adored Pablo Neruda, so we all read his great poem 'The Heights of Macchu Picchu' and I vowed one day I would visit Peru — though by the time I could have, I decided not to, as it was overrun by tourists who came in such numbers it was damaging to the ancient site.

Ian Wedde, Alan Brunton and Russell Haley, who hated that C. K. Stead had once named him *the only Yorkshire surrealist poet in New Zealand*, were in cahoots and had worked together on the little magazine *The Word Is Freed* which Murray had asked me to contribute to as well. Sometimes there were verbal fights among the men: opinionated, young, certain of themselves, of their art and way of it, their tongues mightier than their fists. They'd argue and contradict and discuss and drink (mostly beer) on and on into the night, sitting on the floor of the tiny living room at, say, Russell and Jean's house, wrangling. I wrote them a poem which, along with a few others, Murray first published in *Freed*.

The icemen

Where do they all go?
these dealers in ice —
pitching back & forth
the jarred pick
stabbing at stunned ice-rock.

Recall — the stone blunts the scissors
recall — a blunt knife splints desperate scratches
on wedge-thick glass
recall — a keen blade knifes sharp through flesh
the wound knits well, leaving but the thinnest line —
a trace of fine cut:

a man and a man with rounded swords
fight a dubious battle —
sometimes the sun may thirst for the ice-rock,
drink in cool delicious flow;
the pick will fall from the hand
& maybe the man will stand near the man
& take the heat
& take it slow.

But who was I to try to tell them how to behave? In what I thought was a gentler, more understanding, more loving and female way? I too used ampersands and as much lower case as I could, as we'd been taught to by David Mitchell, anti-intellectual and anti-establishment as he was. We were making our own stand against the line-up of older white male poets and writers, Allen Curnow, C. K. Stead, Kendrick Smithyman et al., who ruled the roost and set the tone. They were New Zealand Poetry incarnate.

We were the young New Zealand poets and wanted to be recognised as such. Students flocked to our readings. And we heard from those who had Wellington poet friends like Ian Wedde that the old rivalry between Auckland and Wellington didn't have to be carried on any longer in the way that Baxter and others had known it. Rhys Pasley and his fellow poets invited us to come to Wellington on the overnight train, to be met and put up at the various poets' houses and flats, so that we could all read together at Downstage Theatre as the 'Late Late Show' after the play of the evening at 11 p.m.

Johannes was against it. *Just you and all those male poets together on the train overnight and staying a night together in Wellington?* But I had some small savings now from my teaching. I too was a poet. It was something I had been given to do. The others were my fleet brothers. Nothing was going to stop me going and doing it — no Johannes, no nothing. I was going *to ride to shoot and to hunt like Melanion* or I would have been no Diana.

A few of us decided to have a practice run by driving in various cars to Hamilton to have a rehearsal there. We all piled out at David Mitchell's brother Stewie's house, ate the meal he'd prepared for us, had our poetry reading and spent the night. There weren't enough beds for everyone, so Murray and I slept in our travelling clothes, and shared a mattress, half in a cupboard with our legs and feet poking out of it.

A few weeks later, we gaily hired sixpenny pillows at the train station in Auckland — it was going to be a long journey. There were seven or eight of us, including Arthur Baysting and his dark-haired wife Jean, the artist. Mary Paul didn't come as she was looking after the baby, Jacob.

The train stopped often, including at Huntly where we got out to stretch our legs and have a cup of tea and someone called out, *Mercer!* and quoted the famous A. R. D. Fairburn line *the squalid tea of Mercer is not strained* — we all knew Shakespeare wouldn't have minded at all. It was a long trip, some of us trying to nap, having slept only intermittently in Hamilton. Waking again, we'd chat or change seats to sit with someone else, then fall asleep again until finally we arrived at Wellington Station.

It was early in the morning. Time enough to get something for breakfast at the just-opening pie cart outside the station and make our way to our various digs all over town. Time for a shower and a change of clothes and a look around Wellington, a visit the Weddes' house on the hill, then gathering for dinner downtown. At about 10 p.m. we were at the door of Downstage, being shushed into silence by the usher because the play hadn't yet ended, then shown into a waiting vestibule where all the coats were hanging. Half an hour later the clapping inside the auditorium ended and people filed out of the theatre, looking at us as if we were rather odd to be sitting there waiting for something, like Godot. Indeed, we were. And unlike with Godot, something happened.

Downstage had a restaurant as well as a small stage, so we sat in a semi-circle on that raised dais, with the audience, in pairs or fours, sitting slightly below us at small round tables with red-checked cloths and little lamps with even smaller red checks on their shades, each with a tiny chain with which to pull the light off and on so they could see their dinners and drinks.

It was good for us to have the stage spotlights, one haloing each poet as we read, for we needed them to shine on our manuscripts in that dark, clubby atmosphere. We were each given five minutes. When the light fell on me, I stood up and walked to the lectern and spread out my papers on it. Always better to keep your hands free — I am a bit of a gesticulator when I read or talk.

I first read the little love poem 'Puriri' to get them used to my voice. Then a longer poem, 'City sequence', whose setting, I explained to the audience, actually begins in Wellington — my having learned from the Arts Centre readings to introduce a poem with a few words so as to orient the listener — and even tells of a visit I made to

Wellington a few years earlier, determined like so many young woman students, to *lose my virginity*, though like many biographical details let loose, somehow it's a story embedded in the poem's texture, which could be read as truth or fiction.

The poem winds over five rambling pages, and documents time spent in both Wellington and Auckland from high school age, when I first took trips in the brown Howick bus to sit in the Auckland City Library, pretending to read, but watching, learning, listening, observing, taking it all in, life, the bigger picture, the world beyond family and school and hometown. Learning from experiencing life. That is what I wanted to do, so that I'd begin to know it as it is.

City sequence

I

In one city / you can stride / from one side / to the hill /
without wetting your feet / or getting headshrunk — / it
is not her city / she walks on the town / takes it under her
feet — / the Eskimos live in a cold land / wear ice for shoes
/ she's tall as your chalk towers / your secret shops — /
She first lay in you / the sign on his door / graphic design
/ the window opens / the dark night of the city / come let
us die! /

II

In the other city — / suck your fingers in the bus / taking

you to town / tentative girl / the dull library / holds all fiction to you — / you sit amongst musk odour / shy from the men with eyes / never really reading — / tentative trips after school. /
The boy who sat at the films / his hand under the girl's hair / the nape shape of love / his house led on / room to spare room, / drawn on the wall — poems, directions 'madness is infinite perception' / it troubled you — / one night you waited / reading Huxley on a mescaline mattress / the black iron banister / lithe and slippery / he talked / on concrete walls & staircases / you took him all in. / Will he? will he? Willie Willy the taxi driver / take me straight home / embroider Jay on your tea towels aunty / then wrap the scones up / I will take them through the forest! / The children cut / paper houses / glue them on / write underneath: this is our city full of houses / I like the city / It is not raining in our city / it is sunny.
Oh, you vain girl / to go collecting images like pieces of rain / — verbal panacea. /

III

All roads lead into the city / the hub, / humdrum nexus-point. / On sabbatical Saturday the Islanders come / in black & white / to worship the dead opposite / of their coloured sarong Sunday / SUN DAY / you tired city — / take peace in the park of you — / people do — / flap your skirt up, up, / show your thighs, / devise — / nothing: the ground O proven over & over / don't take her / on her

surface face / she hasn't really got one /
the back-track mind glimpses: / califont's off dear / the girl
steps into the street / takes baths / at separate appointed
houses — / while you make pikelets in the attic / the
house up the road burns down / cover their belongings in
green plastic / save on water damage.

IV

Her time is not yet — the tall man hunched in the door /
delighted in telling her / the take of Chanticleer the cock /
that his hen never knew / the boy who made candles
through the wall / the supreme Arabian woman / who
simply sat and moved you / the black-haired bicycle lady /
wore a waterproof canopy / took off like a balloon; / they
spoon-fed you / indiscriminate flashes. / Take the steps
with your feet / feeling the trailing gum strips, / light your
firecrackers on the pavement / roll with him in a wooden
hoop / stand on the brink of a wall & shriek: / I am not all /
of this gully! / The pacifist / isn't merely passive; he wants /
some factual piece of you / you & her / to tell him / it's
blown over / doesn't want you / to stutter like some lost
leaf / in the gutter / on an empty wind. /

V

What are you doing / under the bonnet of my car /
mechanic? /
I want to ride on the city / I won my / rocking horse in a
raffle. /

The road runs out of a city — / take it when you will; / don't let this scant dilettantism fox you / you are still prone / as your voice makes you. / She walks on the town / takes it under her feet / she's tall as your hawk towers / your private shops / the window opens / the dark night of the city.

The rocking horse of the poem was my husband Johannes, whom as Johannes Maris Caris, I'd married. I was myself now Janet Mary Caris (I'd changed my name, because *carissimi* means dearest in Italian, or *splendid* in Greek — both thoughts I loved). It seemed I had found some security after all the adventures of adolescence and growing up just a little. But was that true?

The audience loved it — my reading also, standing up there on stage declaiming the spoken word as I so loved doing, feeling always I was born to do this. This was my thing.

All of us were soundly cheered, from intellectual Ian Wedde and witty Bill Manhire to Murray and Bob and Russell Haley with his surrealist images and sometimes shouting antics, spinning off Alan Brunton's acerbic asides. We were a hit. The next day there was a headline in the *Dominion*: 'The Young New Zealand Poets Come Out at Downstage Theatre'. Arthur Baysting had been given both an epithet and the title for the book he would publish with Heinemann in 1973. It included eighteen male poets and me.

To celebrate after the reading, we all found our way to a house on one of the Karori hills for a great party, full of young long-haired people, ourselves included, full of wine, beer, some cheap spirits, dope of all kinds — marijuana, hashish, whatever anyone had smuggled in — and loud rock music. We danced madly with one another, and when we were leaving to return to whatever digs we had, I saw two girls struggling with each other outside in the grassy dirt off the veranda, trying to tear the other's hair out — a cat fight, as they say. Perhaps they were fighting over the same young man. Who did he belong to? It was a sad end to a happy, wild evening.

The next day many of us took the steep tram trip on the cable car up from Lambton Quay to Kelburn and walked over the top of the hill down to the Botanical Gardens, where others joined us to experience its phantasmagoria, including, at the Begonia House, a flower I'd never before seen. When I got back to Titirangi, I tried to put the whole weekend experience into my poem.

In the Begonia House

The shell on your ear is the sea / cochlea beach of the
whorled elk horn fern / in that hot house of lush / the
begonia house where we / prefer green orchids to red, / for
green flowers are rare. / Taste the orchid grass / on your
tongue / it shows you the oriental brush / strokes but once.

Once you enter / the glass plate dome, / you have a choice: /
to stay / in the hot splash of colour / smudged on green /
spiced sultry soil / or to leave / for the circular garden /
where patterns / are nicely placed / & the roses pruned /
back to bent sticks / every season.

We choose to stay / to hear the trumpet — / cacophonic
echoes / in the tunnel / trumpet phallus / of the elk horn
& green antlers / & the fecund calyx: / we choose to sit /
under the dome — / stop the sun clock / with a stare in
the dark / at the wolves' eyes: / yet in this nether world, /
the plants tend to / sap our eyes, / envelop our shapes /
with their iridescent / flex green lashes / in grotesque
carnival. / Les biches claw at each other's eyes / crawl over
the carpet / to bury themselves / in the dirt.

We cannot turn back / to the circular garden / we cannot
hear the beach / nor smooth the stones into our hands /
we can only prefer green orchids / know the singular
stroke of the brush — / we forgot to look at begonias.

Philosophically, I was trying to say we don't know why we are alive. We have the choice to try to find out, but maybe we'll assume wrongly, and we'll never know. It's my writing back to Nietzsche, when Zarathustra says, *Also, Gott is tot* (Therefore, God is dead), not because I think so but because I don't know, yes or no.

Back in Auckland we were hot news. One of the poets who knew R. A. K. Mason, the earliest of the poets in the great *Mason Glover Fairburn Curnow Brasch* tradition, and mentor to Hone Tuwhare, arranged for us to meet and read with him. Instead, one week later, I attended Ron's funeral and wrote him this farewell poem after watching Curnow, Stead and the other male literati filing into the Maclaurin Chapel where Johannes and I had got married. I wasn't so keen on titles in those days, or couldn't dream them up, so just called it 'Poem'.

Poem

for R. A. K. Mason

I come unasked to your funeral.
The solemn men, dark-coated,
your friends, give you their pass to heaven
by a natural door.
We were to have lauded you
you died a week too soon.

From where I stand on the edge
I hear your words they read.
Through the windows of the chapel,
I see cabbage-tree flax,
flat & flex
licking the blue sky,
a whip in a green wind.

Later, I braved up the courage to phone Ron's widow, Dorothea Mason, who lived, as Frank Sargeson did, in Takapuna on the North Shore. She was very welcoming, accepted my poem very graciously and giving me a cup of tea. Then she showed me a treasure she'd discovered behind the clock on their mantelpiece: a small envelope from Ron, inscribed by him — *for Dorothea, to be read in the event of my death* — and inside it the note: *My dear, do not grieve for me too long. Yours ever, Ron.* How touching it was to have met her and that she read me such precious words.

Of our group, Russell Haley had become my 'older-poet brother' — we got on so well just talking, even though he was forever telling me I was so middle class and should somehow not be. I didn't really know much about class anyway. As Kiwis we were encouraged to think of ourselves as all equal to everyone else. What is class? Russell, as he explained patiently, deliberately dropping the *H*, was born lower-middle class in 'uddersfield in Yorkshire; he'd had a job as a tram conductor and met his wife Jean, who I knew slightly as the librarian at Auckland Teachers' College, and who was lower-lower-middle, while clipping her tram ticket.

They'd been together ever since and had two young children, Ian and Cathy, each with a shock of fair hair like Jean's own. They lived in their own house, a villa in Mount

Eden where, if ever you called in to say hello, there'd be a cup of tea and talk and a roll-your-own cigarette at the drop of a hat. Russell thought of himself as a writer through and through, though he'd had umpteen other jobs, most recently as a postman, and it was Jean whose steady income mostly kept the family on track, supplemented by their huge back yard vegetable garden full of the rich soil from the volcano Mount Eden had once been.

Russell had been corresponding with the American poet Robert Creeley, who was considering one of Russell's stories for publication in *New Directions*, the prestigious US literary journal. Russell was over the moon with joy. Over yet another pot and cups of tea in the large kitchen-cum-dining room he told me all about the American Beat poets like Allen Ginsberg and that he, Russell, had done lots of his own *howling* in his poems but was really a prose writer — short stories were his thing.

As for me, he wondered if I'd heard of Jung's description of the human mind, with some things being in shadow in the unconscious, either collective or personal, and some not; that there was a horizon above which things showed, below which they were hidden. In my case, he said, I showed myself to the world in my poems through my emotion and senses, but he could see that behind it I had an intellect which gradually, as I developed, would one day come more to the fore.

I hoped so. And believed him and observed myself acutely. So many people said to me, *But you have no covering; you present your Self to the world; you need a protective mask.* But how to develop one? I had no idea. I just knew, if I met someone on the street who said, *I loved your little poem about the puriri moth,* that I felt as if they could see right through me and out the other side. I was so transparent. The only thing for me to do was to keep running and ducking behind the lamppost of the next poem-to-be, then peeking out and saying, *See, it's not me, I wrote this new poem yesterday . . . I'm further down the track now, you can't catch me.* And on. A terrible game of hide and seek.

But I did know I wanted to be a poet above all. Having so admired Dave Mitchell, I visited him a couple of times in his room in the house he shared with the gentle Barry Lett, who ran Barry Lett Galleries on Lorne Street, at the end of a Mount Eden cul-de-sac. In his almost bare room, David had a sleeping mattress covered by a pillow or two and some bedclothes, a corner wardrobe made of a stick on the diagonal with some coat-hangers on which hung a few clothes, and a three-cornered wooden stool on which he sat before the high plank which served as a desk.

On the plank were a great sheaf of papers and his little typewriter. He was putting together a collection entitled *Pipe Dreams in Ponsonby* and knew almost all the poems by heart, as he was always presenting them at readings or quoting them to himself, or making up new ones, as if muttering; or he would break into one in the middle of a conversation — raising his voice and pitch a little, as if switching into poetic mode. I adored him because of his total commitment. I also adored his belt, his slimness, his jeans, his poverty, his dedication. We made love on his mattress, and I thought I'd found my true partner at last.

But no. David had had, and would have, many more partners, one or two he would write yearning poems about, but he was always moving on. Shattered by the experience, I wrote what later became the title poem of my first book *Against the Softness of Woman*, published in 1976 by Caveman Press in Dunedin. Though all the poems in it were written and submitted to him by the end of 1972, the publisher Trevor Reeves stalled on releasing it for some years, as he wasn't certain a book solely by a woman poet would sell.

Against the softness of woman

Vagrant woman, pawn your Piscean flood,
don't wave your flower, keep your blood dry
as the gaze behind your eye —
let the resilient bitch rise in the belly of your skies
& face it without your usual vacillation.

You were born to fit him
to be his lay, his lie
his way to run his way.

When he has pared down his spare image
don't try to catch him / you'll catch yourself.
Don't let the quick spring flow,
hide it behind: cut your / lip-service, your idolatry —
he has bared himself translucent
like the rings of honesty:
don't be the dry pip between his petals
he will spit you out.

When you are sunk tight on the pain,
let his singularity teach you:
soften your gall. It wanes thin
held in the light:
transparency holds no mystery:

become like him —
wear your other heart on your other sleeve
keep this one boned down fine.

I'd been dumped. Yes. But so had many women. And the poem told our story. It was very flattering to men. So far, I wasn't much of a feminist. I had a copy of Germaine Greer's *The Female Eunuch* with its stylised woman's body like a singlet on a coat-hanger on the cover, but I never read it; I wasn't good at reading prose, especially if it was polemic. Russell was quite right: my intellect was still in abeyance, waiting in my subconscious until such time as it came over the horizon and showed itself. I did later realise that my title was a *double entendre*. How unwittingly clever of me.

That's the kind of thing a poet really rejoices in when we read what we've written. Just like Griffy, Arthur Baysting, too, had always advised, *Get the poem down. Just write it. Let your mind work on it later and finesse it. Then read it and see what you've written.*

4.

I knew I would have to leave Johannes. I couldn't bear his harangues any longer about how women had it so much better than men did; we could go to a concert bare-shouldered, showing our bodies, whereas a man had to be dressed, had to cover his up; we could lie by our swimming pools all day (not that we had one), while the husbands went out to work and brought home the money. On it went. I couldn't stand it any longer. I was starting at last to think for myself.

Next door to David Mitchell in Mount Eden lived kindly red-haired Malcolm Fraser and his teacher wife Frances, and their two little girls. They had a spare room, with a small study leading off it, with windows looking up the steep bank towards the street. I could rent it from them and park my Baby Austin on the roadside at the top of the entrance above the steps, no problem.

So, in the May holidays of 1972, I moved out of Johannes's house, having spent a first term at the University of Auckland in the MA class, taking all seven papers in English because I was sure I'd never be able to write an academic thesis. Johannes was livid. All the old arguments: *I never wanted to marry in the first place. If you hadn't got mixed up with those poets, you wouldn't leave. It's all your fault it went wrong — you were able to attract more lovers than I could.* But I couldn't bear it any longer. I wrote him a special poem, guilty as I was for having hurt him so.

A pattern of loving

I

With my fingers on your face
I trace your pattern
stencilled deep in the soft fabric of your skin:
I cannot cut you out
& paste you like
some gaudy poster on the fence
& let you flap
& watch you tear apart.
We have held hands
too long for that —
the very pith of you

has patterned me to this pitch:
from this focus fan out
to where we stand single —

II

I wear pitch-black
in my labyrinth
for my voice is my lantern,
& pluck pieces of people
& place them about me:
but I pay what I owe
for each face that I pick,
for like returns like
& love begets love
& love regrets loving
at this pitch —

III

You place your fingers on my face
& trace my pattern
in the soft fabric of my skin:
can you cut me out & paste me
like some gaudy poster on the fence
& let me flap & let me tear apart?

IV

We have held hands too long for that.
The very pith of me has fashioned you

to this pitch.
Then let us stand single
& spare ourselves, apart
in our own labyrinths
where love can let love at this pitch.

As someone once said of the title poem of this first book, *Purple writing, vatic stuff!* Quite right. But with audiences, especially from women, such poems drew immediate response. They knew what I was talking about, even if I wasn't nearly as skilled as, say, Russell or David in saying it. The poems were heartfelt. And, though it's no excuse at all, I was just twenty-two years old, with much still to learn about both life and art.

One of our lecturers was the dark-haired, intense, handsome and tall, almost gypsy-looking, Terry W. We were to read W. H. Auden with him. And remembering Anna Marsich's wonderful reading with us in English I and Auden's poem 'Musée des Beaux Arts', I attended his lectures.

Somehow or another Terry and I befriended each other. He found he could talk to me, which he couldn't do with his girlfriend, who was so closed, except in bed he said, where they matched each other in a grand passion. So how it came to be that he and I slept together I can't say. But she hung over me like a spectre. And Terry was somehow so urgent, troubled, with so much from his soul to unburden, I wondered if I could manage at all.

I had a lovely room at Malcolm and Frances's with pale-lavender wallpaper and a large double bed; a quiet room looking out onto the lush flax in the garden between our house and Barry Lett's. I pretended David was never there when I looked out the window. I had to get on with my life. But again, it seemed I'd made a mistake. I wrote three poems for Terry. A slightly witty happy one —

Candle

The flame is a tongue —
lick caress,
strident forking
into narrow strips of air:
at times lizard-like,
shoot & suck back
consummate:
his black wick bends —
her alabaster wax dissolves —
the candle makes love with itself:
he leans over, lights
two cigarettes from the flame.

And a pair of poems, 'Hexandra in recess' (the name just came to me, though I vaguely remembered reading that Hexandra was a prophetess) and '"By woman wailing for her demon lover"', written in that lilac peacock-feather-coloured room, telling of loss and frustration. He'd gone back to his girlfriend.

Somehow, the poems were published in the poems' pages of the *New Zealand Herald* entitled *The Lost Loves of Hexandra*, with a soppy photo of me and a review of them by the critic Stephen Chan, who pronounced that *this poet will transcend the narrow borders this country provides.* I was over the moon. And, despite *love lost*, Terry and I still talked to each other. He was greatly impressed when I showed him the two poems. *I didn't realise*, he said. *You must continue. You must write. These are incredibly good.* Well, he had once been the editor of *Craccum*, so he ought to know. And he taught poetry.

Hexandra in recess

Cover those blind bland eyes
with clay & spittle —
let the mud cakes dry
cracked & brittle
that dust may flake
into the giddied air,
dance & dissolve.
Between flesh of thumb & finger
ash-flakes become a mere rub:
crushed leaves smear
the sap & cool stain

of green or purple on skin:
she sniffs at mint or violets,
lets the tinted fingers
touch gentle her hot eyes.
She plucked a peacock's feather —
all he did was strut & bloom;
now the glancing turquoise eye
dances echoes in her silver room.

'By woman wailing for her demon lover'

No smoky incubus nor swan
is steed for this Hexandra —
riding time's night, bareback
Godiva of the sheets:
after the bullwhip cracks
the air in slivers
after the tiered planks are hush,
she will still ride, ride
circling the ring, thud hooves
scudding sawdust on sweating flanks
molten in floodlight,
apparition
for her gipsy's sight alone:
then, she will kiss his eyes
as he once anointed hers.

Now Terry was wanting to write a film script. *You are a writer*, he said. *I'm writing a film script, but I just can't do dialogue. Would you work with me on the script?* Indeed, I would, though it would mean that in the holidays I'd need to move to the sprawling farmhouse he'd rented outside the city.

Terry got a group of us together, including Alan Smythe as his PR man, a sound man, a camera man, some possible actors — though later I thought who could better play Terry, dark and brooding, than Terry himself? But he was directing, and most probably wasn't a good actor because he couldn't play anyone else, and besides that he didn't want to be photographed.

I was given my own room in the house. It was on and off again with Terry in the sense that, though we were considerate and close, depending on each other as friend and colleague, it didn't work for me in the Lawrentian, doggedly speechless way his passion with his previous girlfriend had functioned. Nor for him, I suppose. He rammed and rammed me and said, *But you don't come.* Well, I wonder why not. I think, despite the Coleridgean *woman wailing* poem, I'm a gentle lover. And she was always there in his mind, hanging over me, over Terry and over the film.

Ali Smythe had become a kind friend. He was staying in the little bach down at the beach nearby. Like me, he was going to join the MA class when university began again in March. And in the following year (after I'd got back from sailing in the South Pacific) we became wonderful working partners on the making of the Waiata Archive 1974 — fifty-one New Zealand poets reading their work on three LPs with covers designed by Pat Hanly for the double LP, and by my old friend Michele for the album for children.

Meantime, I went on a fast — a whole week-long fast. I'd sit next to Terry and the film crew at the dining table at each meal but only sipped water. Until I saw a green moth that wasn't there. Worried I was hallucinating, Terry got me to have some soup and the next day a slice of toast and some cheese, and gradually I returned to normal eating habits. But joy of joys, I'd lost half a stone and felt clear-headed.

I knew I'd need to move out and back to the city after the holidays and the filming was done. Wonder of wonders, Johannes helped me move my things, loading up and driving the few pieces of furniture and suitcases and me to Ponsonby. So, he still had a feeling of responsibility towards me, perhaps because he was twenty-two years older?

1972

—

1974

1.

The small cottage at 23 Collingwood Street, with its white filigreed veranda and bay window and where I moved into the front room, sharing the house with another MA student, Evelyn Davis, still stands in Ponsonby. My room looked onto the veranda and the quiet street and downhill to the faraway harbour.

Parking his beach buggy outside the house, Terry would sometimes call in for urgent discussions about the progress of the film. It wasn't going so well. He'd got bogged down with the financing and whole flow of it, and Geoff Steven had come in to take over to help get it finished. It was to be called *Silent Pictures* and would in the end indeed be a silent film.

One evening Terry and I sat in my room together and, his outpouring of sorrows over, we looked down the steep hill through the back window. Way away in the distance could see the lights of the *Oriana*, which was soon to set sail for England. I knew the Haleys were on board — sailing home on a trip to see Jean's parents. They'd be back but still, they were leaving. In a flash Terry and I were in the beach buggy and parking it near the wharf; we were on board and inspecting the Haleys' third-class cabin, then back on the wharf waving and waving, throwing out paper streamers and calling, *Bye! Goodbye! Have a good trip! Come back safely!* My cheeks were wet with tears.

Someone had arranged for a photographer to come to the house. John Miller's 1972 portrait shows me sitting on my high bed near a corner lamp draped under a netted cloth and in front of a huge *Vogue* poster of a woman riding a peacock. I'm looking suitably poetical and contemplative, a cigarette burning in my right hand. I was then, unfortunately, still a dedicated smoker.

Arthur Baysting had asked me to write a preface to the six of my poems he had selected for *The Young New Zealand Poets*. Not only did he want a three-line biodata, but he also wanted to know why each poet wrote — enough text to fill a page. I found it so hard to talk about; it's just something I did without thinking. In fact, I needed to stop trying to think when I wrote, to just listen and try to record what I heard in my head. Eventually, I sent him this:

Born Hamilton 1949. Lives in Auckland. Has been a teacher. Now studying for MA in English. Has taken part in readings in Auckland and Wellington and has read her work on the YC Poetry programme.

to write because of instinct to write is enough / images & ideas spring from things noticed & sensed that is things lived / after it is written you feel the poem had 2 lives — its formless one & now the formed life / organic too, it lives / it is itself . . .

sometimes words, phrases sound out their rhythms in your ear / the title Hexandra in Recess — for instance / Hexandra is a name made up or heard & she seemed to be right — to discover later the links between the word hex & witches & that Cassandra was a prophetess strengthens the sense that a latent, formless pool of idea & images lies behind a poem like that / a sense of a poetic mystique / reinforced by other elements in the poem / links between colours chosen, one image & another / the internal movement that drives a poem to its end & yet keeps it whole . . .

poems as faces of the poet facing, as a revolving glass, the only things there are: what is outside what is inside him / there is no clear delineation / in the end it is a fusion of both / the glass must be transparent, lucid, not muddied / held up to the light the tones through the glass change, as moods shift / so each face remains constant only to that

> face, as each moment exists only for that moment / if you are there then & then — live in totality then & then you can recall the stimuli of the time & use it in the making of another face . . .

I even called the poet *him*. These days I'd write *her*.

Next door to the Collingwood Street house and off the pathway that went below ours and in another small colonial cottage lived Simon D, supposedly a great scholar, who later moved to Australia. In the other room in our house, and with the kitchen between us, lived my flatmate — the tall, leggy, long-blonde-haired, often-laughing Evelyn Davis, daughter of a British potter Harry Davis, who with his young family had immigrated to New Zealand. One day Evelyn held up a pomegranate she'd bought at the Pacific Island market on Ponsonby Road, a short walk up the hill from our house. I'd never seen one before. She then taught me how to eat it — by taking a long needle and picking out and eating the luscious dark-red kernels one by one. Nowadays I sprinkle some on my daily salad.

Evelyn loved to talk — she just held forth in a way I couldn't, very openly and joyously and cleverly. She'd come into my room, thump my desk with a laugh and say *Listen to this*, and I couldn't deter her, even if I too had an essay to write. No, she was leader of the pack and must be heard. So, I listened as she read from her scrawled essay notes and tried to make helpful comments. Then she'd go to the kitchen and crash around making herself and her newly acquired boyfriend Peter some dinner. Peter just adored her, Peter with his curls and Waitākere workman's sloppy clothes, Peter with his slightly hoarse and laughing voice. I could hear them on and on into the night — teasing, laughing, cajoling, then silence . . . they must have fallen asleep or been making love.

The next morning I'd go to the kitchen to make breakfast and have to clear up the mess — all the unwashed plates and cutlery, pots and pans. Why did I? For the sake of peace. I wasn't very good at confronting. And in the end, after a whole year living with Evelyn's obvious MA brilliance — she came out of it with a first-class Honours in English — I decided not to sit, but to wait another year. I truly wasn't ready. Luckily, during the year she had introduced me to someone in our MA class, her old pal Olavi P-K, and my life and place of abode were to change yet again.

Olavi's girlfriend, Alice, a very hard-working medical school student, shared a commodious Parnell house near Queen Victoria School for Maori Girls. She and her flatmate Marian used to let me come and play the piano whenever I wanted, mostly during the day when I was sick of lectures and books and study. Though very studious, Alice loved sharing in Olavi's experimental drug escapades and could smoke dope and enjoy it in a way I really couldn't.

She was perfectly happy about my friendship with

Olavi and once said, *You two are of one mind.* Olavi and I felt indeed we were. He would make an aperçu and I'd understand. All about reality. For by then we had each been accepted into Allen Curnow's prestigious Monday-morning Wallace Stevens class. We were to read Stevens together over the whole year, just seven of us.

With Roger Horrocks as our lecturer, I was enrolled in the first Film course ever offered at the University of Auckland. I also enrolled in Sebastian Black's Twentieth-century Drama, Wystan Curnow's Nineteenth-century American Novel, and Jonathan Lamb's Twentieth-century American Novel course, because I'd already read and written an essay on Saul Bellow's *Henderson the Rain King*, which Jonathan had highly approved of, though probably because of some wild association I'd made, rather than any real knowledge of Bellow's art. How we all loved our great teachers.

Olavi lived in a flat in Wakefield Street and on Sunday night before the Monday morning Curnow/Stevens two-hour-long tutorial, he'd take an acid trip and read the poem we were to discuss — 'Bouquet of Belle Scavoir' or 'The Emperor of Ice-cream', perhaps. I could somehow see the images as Olavi did, though without acid. We laughed and joked and mocked, quoted, and adored Stevens and read him aloud. Then on Mondays in the class Allen Curnow would ask, *And what do you think, Mr P-K?* Or *And what do you think, Mrs Caris?* And slowly we'd all inch our way line by line through the poems. When we stumbled, he'd say, slowly turning and leafing through an accompanying book on his desk, *Let's see what Hi Simons has to say about this.*

Then he'd take up yet another match, light it and try to light his pipe, which had lain neatly in front of the book and quite near us, all seven of us half disappearing below his desk into the lounge chairs borrowed from the English Department senior common room that we somehow fitted into his study, dutifully returning them afterwards. After all, the staff might need them at lunchtime, and those of us in Wystan's evening class in the staff common room needed them too.

How amazing to hold an evening class! Wystan sometimes wore his leather flying helmet with its earflaps. We could bring wine, and Wilton Rodger used to bring a cask and someone else a bottle, others some nuts and crackers, and we'd use the staff plates and wine glasses and wash them up afterwards.

A two-hour discussion on an aspect of nineteenth-century American fiction, perhaps Melville's *Bartleby, the Scrivener* and why he said *I would prefer not to* — a line I've never forgotten, having most of my life felt I ought to. How wonderful to say that other line! A very polite refusal. Not compliance. What a new idea.

2.

Dad had come across a black 1948 Ford Anglia Deluxe motorcar with separate headlights and green leather seats. Having bought it for $150, he presented it to me with much pride and joy. I immediately named it 'Ganymede', after Goethe's poem.

Olavi had found a small half-cottage to let at 1 Cowie Street in Parnell, and we decided to go flatting together. I was to be in the front sunroom off the living room, overlooking the short side street beyond our little front garden with its red-hot pokers under the windows, and he in the bedroom down the hallway, past the kitchen before you got to the bathroom and laundry.

Next door, through the long dividing wall, lived a family — Simon and Marion and their young son, still crawling about. Simon, a steady family man a few years older than us, was employed at Auckland University in a technical studies department. But like Olavi he had a soft spot for experimenting with drugs, and they shared their purchases of marijuana, hashish and acid. I caught wind of this but wasn't present at their deals.

As for Olavi himself, how best to describe him? Perhaps Olavi too was a Ganymede, a Pan figure — you could imagine his pipe, though he wasn't a bit musical.

A Narcissus too, really — very slender and smooth-skinned and laughing, and not taking life at all seriously, it seemed, but all the time examining himself very closely. Life's a joke! He was phantasmagorical. He was metaphorical. His mind was the place he explored, as if it were a planet, a castle, a universe unto itself. And his tool to access all there is to access through it, his body.

When we first moved into the flat, we had just our mattresses from Airedale and Collingwood Streets on the floor of the living room. And my faithful old radiogram and some records. Olavi offered to share a joint with me, and I took two or three puffs. We put on Corelli's *Concerti Grossi* and lay there on the mattresses listening. I could see the music in huge circular waves behind my shut eyes, one after another wave of sound transformed into colour and shape — the shapes danced and intertwined as if ballet dancers with long scarves whirling before me — the music moving through our bodies as we lay there inert for the whole first side of the LP. *It's synaesthesia,* I said. *Can you see it too?*

Olavi had a group of firm old friends who used to come round and go into Olavi's room and smoke dope. As I wasn't into it that much, I wasn't really one of them. Though I loved it when a gang of us decided to attend the Joe Cocker concert at Western Springs stadium. I loved Joe's raspy voice and the rock in his beat, the mass of young people madly dancing as we sat, stood and moved in the enormous outdoor space, listening and singing along with Joe. And sometimes we'd go to a house in Herne Bay where Olavi's friend Thomas lived, and gradually Thomas and I struck up some kind of friendship and became lovers while one of the women went off with Olavi.

Thomas loved drugs too but, being a gentle lover, I liked him. He even once said, *Jan's cut lip? No, you never see it. It's the way she uses her mouth, her expressions that I like.* Thanks, Thomas! One day Thomas, Olavi and I were all in Olavi's bed together, Thomas only half agreeing to Olavi's lovemaking, but giving in and turning from one to the other. Not Olavi and me, though. We were of one mind, not one body.

In a tiny garage at the end of our driveway, beyond where Ganymede was parked, lived Sandy, a blond transvestite and junkie. Sandy was melodramatic and full of gestures, loved wearing flashy robes and colour. Some of my junk-shop clothes disappeared from my wardrobe and I'd see Sandy wearing them. Even my leather sandals made by the sandal-maker Alan Beverly, who had learned his trade on the hippie trail through Afghanistan. I didn't have the heart to ask Sandy to give my things back. He used to ponce up to the dairy at the corner of Ayr Street and Parnell Road, distract the shop assistant by asking for something from out of the storeroom and, while she was gone, help himself to whatever wares he could, plunging them into his deep pockets, then paying cheerfully for the little he'd bought.

I learned how to do that trick too, and am most

ashamed to now admit, yes, I did a bit of shoplifting then. I was studying on too little money was my excuse to myself. Now, I don't even pluck a flower from the parks on my walks. Only if something is found might I pick it up, as a given. A fallen rose. A bunch of grapes. A leaf.

One day Olavi persuaded me we'd take Ganymede and fetch Evelyn and drive on out to Whatipu where we'd take an acid trip. I was a bit anxious about the whole adventure, being the driver, but he assured me it would be fine. Evelyn let me wear her great English sunhat festooned with fake flowers, the one she later gave me, and we three lay in the lupins and the sand, and Olavi showed us the stuff he had in his palm. I had the last third, a bit less than each of them, licked off his hand. Then we waited and waited.

I felt as if the distance between us had grown. All afternoon we lay there, watching the clouds scud across the enormous sky, looking out over the wide and getting wider sand to the faraway sea, watching the gulls wheeling and crying — everything seemed more and more stretched, more and more vast and spacious. *You're looking at your own consciousness expanding*, Olavi said reassuringly. I understood.

But it was lonely. The space between each of us, the few words each spoke to the other, took an age to reach you — you could see them written on the air as they floated over to your ears and went in. We laughed at what we said, because taken apart like that most of it didn't make the sense it would have in real time. I imagined we were seeing our own minds as if from far away and from the inside of them through a magnifying glass. I didn't ever take a trip again. I'd got the picture.

But every Sunday night, Olavi would take something or other and come into my room if I was alone. Once we sat on my windowsill, dangling our feet amongst the red-hot pokers outside, discussing reality, Wallace Stevens's favourite topic. After all, we were now in the second half of our MA year with Allen Curnow reading Stevens's 'Notes Toward a Supreme Fiction'. He had wanted to create an idea as great as the idea of God had been for previous generations. What a task. How wonderful to realise even God was a fiction.

A Canadian, Justin F, had arrived on his yacht, the *Bella County*, having sailed across the Pacific from Vancouver with his wife Sandra. Justin was much revered by all the Ponsonby bike shop mechanics — among them Archie, my cousin Judy's boyfriend. Justin wore a thick navy-blue sailor's topcoat and spoke mainly in monosyllables. He was an undoubted leader.

And, though he would never admit it, we all thought he was quite possibly a drug smuggler. Probably just marijuana, sailing it from the Pacific Islands to Aotearoa.

He would sit in the middle of the room in a little house at the top of Curran Street in Herne Bay and hold court, slapping his right knee and laughing if anything really caught his fancy. He was able to keep his word and his silence. A real old man of the sea to look at — tall, blond, with a penetrating gaze.

He took to me immediately and decided I should become his *other woman*. The reality was his visiting me at Cowie Street in my little sunroom. I had a new lover, albeit a married one. Oh dear. He even had a friend paint an *odalisque* portrait of me, lying naked on the couch in the front-room studio in the Curran Street house, that he later took back to Vancouver with him. Later still, a nice woman friend of his I somehow or another met said Sandra had hidden it in the attic of her house. Oh dear, again.

3.

Our finals were looming. We were to write a prepared essay for Wystan Curnow, linking five nineteenth-century American novels. *What shall I call my essay?* I asked Olavi who, never at a loss and despite being stoned, immediately said to call it *The function of the imagination in the ability of the individual to orient himself in a constantly incipient cosmos*. And so, I did. Not noticing I should have said *herself*. Feminism was rife. But I didn't know how to apply it, except to continue writing my own poems, just as they came, even though I lived mostly in a male-dominated world.

Olavi was writing his thesis, 'The Earthy Anecdotes of Wallace Stevens', for which Allen Curnow gave him an A++, thinking it a brilliant work. Olavi laughed off his success — he could easily have gone on and written a PhD and become a university tutor like Anna Marsich or Riemke Ensing, the only job I could imagine I'd love to have. But I wasn't an academic. I didn't like writing in that way, though to pass the exams I had to. Poems were something on the side only. There was no creative writing course then, nor any credit given for having written and performed your poems.

Three bright happy sparks in this second MA year were Michele and my friends Ali Smythe and the Yorkshireman and fine eighteenth-century scholar Jonathan Lamb, who was one of our lecturers. Ali had bought himself a Model T Ford and would collect the three of us from the university, then off we'd go to Piha or Anawhata to laugh, joke, have a walk on the beach, smoke a joint or two, drink a beer, have a picnic, and drive back again. Happy.

As was the day of the Ayr Street poets-and-friends garden party, 16 April 1972, hosted by Arthur Baysting and Jean Clarkson. A knock on the door at Cowie Street, and there stood David Mitchell, all dressed up in a white sports coat with a pink carnation, ready to escort me to the party. What a surprise. I was already dressed in a long, dark-red silk nightie from a Ponsonby Road junk shop where Evelyn and I used to shop, as well as a fluffy fake-fur 'white rabbit' short jacket and a pair of sandals. Delighted with each other, we set off down Parnell Road the few hundred metres to the back garden of the old Tudor corner house at 2 Ayr Street where Arthur and Jean lived. David and I sang Marty Robbins's 'A White Sport Coat and a Pink Carnation' as we walked.

Everyone was there — Russell and Jean Haley, Rodney Fumpston, the painter who'd been at school at St Paul's with my brother Pete, poets like Barry Southam and all. Intense conversations went on the whole afternoon with a steady supply of drinks and food and perhaps some drugs, though I didn't notice them. We all posed for a photograph taken by Jean Clarkson, with our hero, Davy Mitchell, sitting on the grass at the front near someone's dog.

Sitting the MA examination papers wasn't fun at all. Seven papers on different subjects with a three-hour written paper in each. In one of them, I lost my head completely and wrote *that thrush sitting outside and singing on that twig has far more to say than I have here,* and left the room, thinking, I've failed. They can't possibly let me through now.

Imagine it — an MA, albeit an Aegrotat, with Second Class Honours, Second Division . . . I'd passed! But what on earth to do with it? They didn't appoint poets without

Jean, Russell and Ian Haley (partly obscured) and Jan, coming back from the beach at Bethells, 1973. DENIS TAYLOR

doctorates to be tutors or lecturers any longer, as they had done for Kendrick Smithyman and Allen Curnow — and, anyway, I wasn't in their league.

Olavi could have gone on to do a PhD, but that was far too boring for him. Off he flew to Australia, a band of us traipsing to Auckland Airport to see him off. I met him once again, years later, when I was living in Singapore, where I'd frequent the Shangri-La Hotel and sit for hours in the coffee shop writing blue aerogramme letters to family and friends to while away the loneliness and boredom of the weekends.

One day, after leaving my faithful creamy yellow Daihatsu Charade with its backseat portholes in the carpark, I walked up the steps and into the grandiose foyer. I was crossing to the escalator leading to the coffee shop when I suddenly saw him. *Olavi P-K!* I called. *Jan Kemp!* Olavi delightedly bowed and presented his male friend and partner with a flourish. Down we three went to the coffee shop. It was marvellous to see him again. He hadn't changed a bit.

Justin's wife Sandra and I had meanwhile both got jobs in a strawberry patch in Henderson, driving out there in my car in the early mornings to earn some money and staying temporarily in separate spare rooms in the Curran Street house until she could fly to join Justin, who was sailing in Fiji. His arrangement was I should fly there too, and we should set up a *ménage à trois* on the *Bella County*. Sandra would just have to get used to it, as many an Asian wife did, as Justin would say.

When I consulted him about it, Olavi, turning his hands out at his sides as he often did to indicate anything goes, said, *Try it, try anything once! After all, Muslims can even have four wives.* Sandra, though, was livid at the thought of even a second wife. And didn't hide it from me or from Justin.

Eventually a telephone call came from him: *I'm sorry, my girl, Sandra just won't allow it. So, I'm sending you a ticket to fly to Fiji and sail the boat round to Nandi with me. Sandra will then fly to Nandi Airport where I'll meet her, and you'll have to move on. But you'll still be my girl, wherever you are, and one day I'll come and find you.*

At least I had a ticket to fly away and somewhere to go to. At least I would go sailing. At least I wouldn't have to be with Sandra and pick strawberries anymore. So, I packed up a sail bag of old light cotton clothes, Evelyn's hat and an extra pair of oars that Justin needed for his dinghy and flew off to Fiji.

4.

Justin had contacted my former boyfriend Hank, for whom I'd written my puriri moth love poem, who was now living on his own yacht, *Ruakuri*, anchored at Port Vila in the New Hebrides. Not knowing Hank and I had once been close, Justin arranged that I could stay on the *Ruakuri* for a few months so that I wouldn't immediately have to return home to Auckland. My mother wired me the money for the air ticket — dear Joanie — and after Justin and I had sailed *Bella County* round from Suva to Nandi and following Sandra's arrival at Nandi Airport, off I flew in an Air Pacific plane to Port Vila.

There Hank fetched me in his jeep, and took me to the slipway where a few yachts lay gently at anchor a little offshore. He put my bag into the prow of the dinghy, told me to sit down in the middle and, having untied it from its post (a mango tree), stood at the end like a gondolier and scull-steered the dinghy the short distance to the yacht. There he told me I could have the right-hand bunk. I could tell from Hank's coolness there'd be no renewal of our former love affair; I was Justin's girl now. Untouchable. That was fine with me. You don't go backwards.

Les Nouvelles Hebrides/the New Hebrides was the last condominium in the whole world. It had two names, two flags and two currencies. Expatriates and locals who had money daily watched the currency exchange go up and down, and played the stakes, shifting their funds from one currency to the other and back again, depending on the prediction of the day's values.

Soon I found a part-time job as a waitress at the French restaurant *Le Pandanus*, a bus ride around the island from

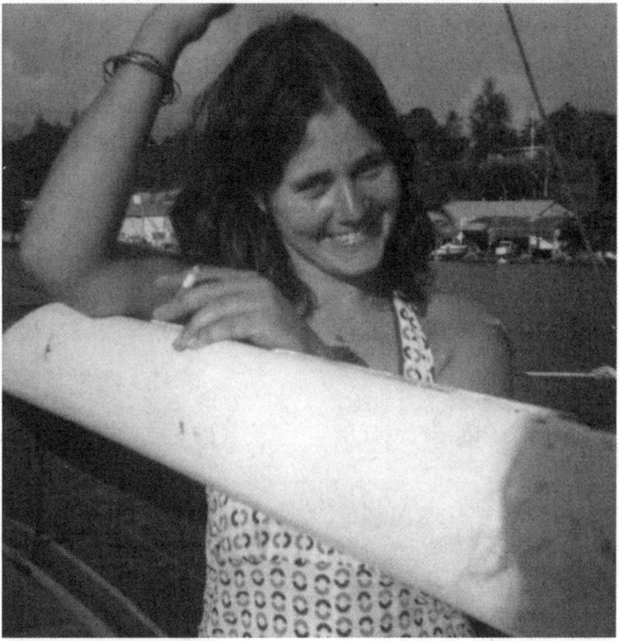

Leaning on the boom of *Te Mariner* while tootling in the harbour at Port Vila, New Hebrides, 1973. ROBYN ARMSTRONG

our anchorage, and would go there about three in the afternoon, returning in the evening, getting home and creeping into my bunk by about 11 p.m. or even midnight if it was a *dinner & dance* night. The head waiter Gerard was French-speaking only, and so were many of the customers — though there were plenty of Australians, some of whom would try to trip you up as you raced out of the kitchen carrying in each hand a huge wooden platter with a sizzling steak. I'd have given their order to the chef as *Deux Chateaubriand, s'il vous plait!*

I longed for Justin to sail in alone and, as I'd dreamed, take me sailing on the Pacific Ocean. Instead, I wrote him a poem.

Seal to the sea captain

At times like this
when the breath
chokes my throat
& I long to see your face
in blue space
& feel you spring within me
& cry out
with the tide's
peak of foam wave broken
& look steep
in the kept part
of your lit eyes —

I know it is
no dream
would wake us
only a sunlit fire
warms us
makes us.

But what to do next? Joanie had not very sensibly posted my MA degree certificate, now issued in my own name *Janet Mary Kemp*, because though we weren't divorced until late June 1974, I'd long since left Johannes Caris and had decided never again to give away my birth name, even if I were eventually divorced and might one day remarry. I picked up a slightly battered cardboard tube at the *Poste Restante* in Port Vila and unrolled the large MA degree certificate with its University of Auckland emblem and seal. Useless for a French-speaking waitress, but so thoughtful of my mother.

As she would be over the divorce case, standing up in the dock and confirming no, I hadn't lived with my husband for the past three years. I didn't have one of my own, so Johannes had reluctantly allowed me to share his lawyer, who told me *Though you have waived your right to half his property, you can never waive your right to maintenance.*

But I had decided I didn't want to take either. To me they were just things. I still had my life ahead of me, and

Johannes had wanted to keep everything. Perhaps, having lost his parents and lived through a war as a schoolboy, what he needed above all was security. He even asked that I pay half the uncontested divorce fee of $300; my parents paid it for me, as I had nothing. I was free of him. A year later, on an impulse, I phoned him and said I was coming to collect two of the four Canadian chairs — my half of a possession I had bought for us both. A small act of defiance. Or an attempt at fairness.

On Friday 15 February 1974, Queen Elizabeth II sailed into the harbour on the Royal Yacht *Britannia* for a two-day visit, accompanied by the Duke of Edinburgh and Princess Anne. The whole island of Efate was agog with excitement, and preparations were made to receive the party on the flat field used for community activities and sports in the middle of Port Vila town, where they would be welcomed by traditional dancers in costume, the place festooned with palm leaves and fronds, colourful leis and tropical flowers.

I heard of the news too late and so decided to skip the gathering and instead make my way down to the jetty, where the royal barge that had brought the Queen onto the island was tied up, waiting to take her back to the *Britannia*. Early as I was, I stood with a gathering crowd of onlookers just behind the cordon, almost opposite some New Hebrideans holding up a huge poster on which they had written in black letters *Go home, you're not our Queen.*

The hot afternoon dragged on, and I was grateful for the shade of a coconut palm frond or two that someone near me was holding. Suddenly a black car drew up and out they got, both the Queen and Princess Anne wearing large hats and Princes Anne's face caked with makeup, shielding her fair skin from the sun. The Duke followed a step or two behind them.

It's a sign of the times, a sign of the times, I heard the Queen say to the others in an ever so slightly resigned but accepting tone of voice as she took in the protestors' sign. Quite right, QE II, so it is, I thought, impressed, as she delicately stepped back down off the jetty onto the polished wooden barge to be seemingly floated back out to the yacht. What style!

5.

I have found a new friend — Robyn, a bright, blonde Australian medical student and would-be eye surgeon doing her final practical work year at the hospital on the island in the middle of the harbour before she graduates. She tells me she's recently met the American sailor Blackie, whose yacht *Demaris Teo* is currently pulled up at the slip in Suva for a paint job. In Fiji Blackie met a UN official who flew him over to Port Vila to sail *Te Mariner*, an old thirty-footer with polished wooden decks and an elegant line, back to Fiji. There the UN official would be able to moor his new purchase in the same bay where he and his wife live in a hotel suite, and she could row out to it in the dinghy to dive and swim off it daily and lounge on its decks in the sun.

Now I know who has just moved in two yachts along from Hank's in our moorage. Robyn introduces me to tousle-haired and indeed black-haired Blackie, who says they really need a third crew member and maybe it could be me. We will each do an eight-hour watch every twenty-four hours, our task being to safely sail *Te Mariner* over the 804 sea miles from Efate to Vanua Levu — almost directly 90 degrees east all the way.

But it is hurricane season. The other yachties living nearby are shaking their heads and turning away when they hear of the plan, thinking it all very foolish. I decide to consult Gerard's girlfriend's mother, a French novelist. In my broken but adequate schoolgirl and now waitress French, I explain my dilemma, and she tells me to make a list of the pros and cons, as you should at any time in life when you need to decide. Then you add up each column and go for the decision with the highest tally.

Blackie and Robyn are thrilled to welcome me as the other deckhand. I'm fearful I might well get seasick, as I did on my father's boss Rob Butcher's launch *Fairmile*, sailing around the Coromandel Peninsula from Auckland to

Whitianga years ago. I think I'll just have to grin and bear it and practise not getting seasick by lying on the bottom of the boat, level with the waves, and letting myself go with it.

Blackie has a copy of the Richard Wilhelm translation of the *I Ching* and a set of yarrow sticks. We three sit around the old polished wooden table in *Te Mariner*'s cabin and consult the oracle. The hexagrams tell us *All will be well and all manner of things.*

Blackie organises supplies including, most importantly for him, a huge wicker basket containing several litres of red wine, cans of corned beef, and local avocados and mangoes. The Port Vilan mangoes from the market are delicious, I know. I have loved mangoes ever since, learning how to cut them so they fold out towards you like golden teeth.

The great day comes, and Blackie sets his Mickey Mouse clock to the correct time, unfolds and spreads out his map onto *Te Mariner*'s table, lays on it his sharpened pencil and his sextant and compass brought over with him from *Demaris Teo*, marks where we are and shows us where we're to head — indeed, 90 degrees eastwards. We weigh anchor and set sail, tootling out of the harbour with the motor running so that we're steady and still vertical, and on out to sea. We know it will take us eight days and nights, that we don't have any self-steering, that if we miss finding Fiji it's a long way to sail to South America.

Repressing such negative thoughts, I half lie back into the bowsprit, hearing the waves gush up on either side of the prow beneath me, as they used to do on the prow of Dad's boat *Joanne* in Mercury Bay as we set out to fish in the waters by the Hole in the Wall.

I watch Blackie and Robyn pottering about on the back deck. Our sails are then unfurled. I see the harbour island slip by, then eventually the whole of Efate slides away out of sight, and there is only the sea, the great blue, wavy, wonderful South Pacific Ocean, and we're sailing on it.

Quiet in the eye

for Blackie and Robyn

I

Weathered sailors, secure in season's shelter,
fall silent as we take a feast of days with
beaujolais in woven baskets, bully beef & avocado
aboard Te Mariner, thirty foot of old boned boat,
tarred slat planks, bevelled brass compass & sun awnings
in hurricane season under tropical Capricorn.
'To sail now is folly' — but we have other signatures:
thrown yarrow stalks guide towards an eastern star.

II

We've seen cyclones while anchored six feet from coral,
& played guitar to pitch-drunk sirens;
we've been battened night-long in shelter of islands,
we've seen water spew scum & weeds ashore,
& emerged as tourists to pick over debris of trees.

We sail three days, watching the compass in turns,
invent gadgets to make us millionaires.
while a skinny barracuda dries, strips salted in the sun.

III

In a day, Tanna lies to the south
& Erromanga some low shoal
whale-backed on a wide ocean;
Efate, west behind trolling lines
gentle & green in its lush hibiscus,
some paradise twig in its teeth,
where Melanesia under pandanus leaves
in open market goes for 10 cents a pound.
A boy lops his trousers or machetes
a coconut for sweet milk in the heat.
In L'Houstalet, beer spills on the silk pants
of a Don Juan: outside his Maserati
gleams through coral dust.
Among pineapples at Mele
a Dunedin pilot plays grand opera
in the shade in a canvas chair,
drinking French perfume.
For Christmas the European prisoner
will have new cell furniture,
& serve dinner guests on the lawn.

IV

Under Venus, the night watcher dreams of sailors,
as they lie day upon night,
wracked by a yacht's hard hammer,
locked below & craving for quiet.
But here, in a mild gale
with steep grey seas curled by a knotted wind,
while riding the cockpit bench,
wheel lashed to ninety degrees,
sails reefed & halyards straining,
the rhythm of the sea burns cold salt hands —
there are only sailors here.

V

Darkness lies over the deep
until dawn when footfall fills the mind.
Clouds castle the disc-horizon.
& the vaults of night open:
here no tall sticks mark the rocks,
no lighthouse sweeps the depth of the place.
Now quiet lies on the unbreathed water
& light changes
are fancies of wind on waves:
the sea is the same the day is the same,
morning & evening are come & gone.

VI

On the eighth day a cormorant
bespeaks calm waters & land.
Unaccustomed air
is touched by the wild
& within,
that silent space
holds no fear.

Notes

1949–1961

p. 50 'A childhood secret', in Jan Kemp, *Dante's Heaven*, Puriri Press, 2006, p. 32.

pp. 55–56 'Best friends', in ibid., p. 31.

1962–1966

pp. 103–4 *The force that through the green fuse drives the flower* . . ., from Dylan Thomas, 'The force that through the green fuse drives the flower', 1938, in *The Poems of Dylan Thomas*, New Directions, 1971.

p. 105 *How splendid in the morning / grows the lily* . . ., from James Elroy Flecker, 'Yasmin (A Ghazel)', c.1916, https://internetpoem.com/james-elroy-flecker/yasmin-poem

p. 105 *For one night / or the other night* . . ., in ibid.

pp. 105–6 'Thrush', in *Pegasus*, Pakuranga College, 1966.

p. 115 *Piping down the valleys wild* . . ., from William Blake, *Songs of Innocence and Experience*, 1789, in Geoffrey Keynes (ed.), *Blake Complete Writings*, Oxford University Press, Oxford, 1971.

1967–1969

pp. 131–32 'The white dove', in Jan Kemp, *Against the Softness of Woman*, Caveman Press, Dunedin, 1976, p. 10.

p. 140 *The black-haired bicycle lady wore* . . ., from 'City sequence', in ibid., p. 12.

p. 152 'Poem', in ibid., p. 51.

pp. 153–53 'Mystics mild: Song', in ibid., p. 27.

pp. 162–63 'Old railway guard', in ibid., p. 56.

pp. 164–65 'Babysitting', in Jan Kemp, *Voicetracks*, Puriri Press, Auckland, Tranzlit, Kronberg im Taunus, 2012, p. 62.

p. 176 'The new people', in *Against the Softness of Woman*, p. 23.

1970–1971

p. 197 'The icemen', in *Against the Softness of Woman*, p. 26.

pp. 201–4 'City sequence', in ibid., p. 12.

pp. 205–6 'In the Begonia House', in ibid., p. 18.

p. 207 'Poem (for R. A. K. Mason)', in ibid., p. 21.

pp. 211–12 'Against the softness of woman', in ibid., p. 9.

pp. 214–16 'A pattern of loving', in ibid., p. 28.

p. 217 'Candle', in ibid., p. 22.

pp. 218–19 'Hexandra in recess' and '"By woman waiting for her demon lover"', in ibid., pp. 24–25.

1972–1974

pp. 226–27 *Born in Hamilton, 1949 . . .*, in Arthur Baysting (ed.), *The Young New Zealand Poets*, Heinemann, Auckland, 1973, p. 65.

pp. 224–45 'Seal to the sea captain', in Jan Kemp, *Against the Softness of Woman*, p. 44.

pp. 250–53 'Quiet in the eye', in Jan Kemp, *Diamonds and Gravel*, Hampton Hunt, Wellington, 1979, pp. 26-27. With special gratitude to Prof. John Newton for rescuing stanza three from the cutting-room floor to where it was assigned in 1979 and restored in 2000 via his recommendation in Alan Brunton, Murray Edmond and Michele Leggott (eds), *Big Smoke: New Zealand Poems 1960–1975*, Auckland University Press, Auckland, pp. 291–94. The poem was first published in Alistair Paterson (ed.), *Contemporary New Zealand Poems*, Pilgrims South Press, Dunedin, 1980.

MASSEY UNIVERSITY PRESS

First published in 2022 by Massey University Press
Private Bag 102904, North Shore Mail Centre
Auckland 0745, New Zealand
www.masseypress.ac.nz

Design by Kate Barraclough

A catalogue record for this book is available from the National Library of New Zealand

Printed and bound in China by Everbest Printing Investment

ISBN: 978-1-991151-14-8
eISBN: 978-1-991016-06-5

creative nz
ARTS COUNCIL OF NEW ZEALAND TOI AOTEAROA

The assistance of Creative New Zealand is gratefully acknowledged by the publisher